KEY
TO
IMMORTALITY

*A Commentary on the Secret Teaching
attributed to Jesus
in the Gospel According to Thomas*

A commentary by

Stanisław Kapuściński

IP

INHOUSEPRESS, MONTREAL, CANADA

Published by
INHOUSEPRESS
1470 St–Jacques, suite 7, Montreal, Qc., H3C 4J4

Design and layout
Bozena Happach

ISBN 978-0-9813015-3-2

Paperback Edition 2014
INHOUSEPRESS

EXCERPTS FROM SOME 5 STAR REVIEWS ON AMAZON KINDLE

Other books by Stanislaw Kapuscinski

DICTIONARY OF BIBLICAL SYMBOLISM
VISULIZATION—Creating your own Universe
DELUSIONS—Pragmatic Realism
BEYOND RELIGION Volumes I
BEYOND RELIGION Volumes II
BEYOND RELIGION Volumes III
[Three Collections of Essays on Perception of Reality]

Fiction by Stan I.S. Law
(aka Stanislaw Kapuscinski)
Novels

WALL—Love, Sex, and Immortality
[Aquarius Trilogy Book One]
PLUTO EFFECT
[Aquarius Trilogy Book Two]
OLYMPUS—Of Gods and Men
[Aquarius Trilogy Book Three]
YESHUA—Missing Years of Jesus
PETER AND PAUL—Intuitive Sequel to Yeshûa
MARVIN CLARK—In Search of Freedom
GIFT OF GAMMAN
ENIGMA OF THE SECOND COMING
ONE JUST MAN [Winston Trilogy Book One]
ELOHIM [Winston Trilogy Book Two]
WINSTON'S KINGDOM [Winston Trilogy Book Three]
THE PRINCESS
GATE—Things my Mother told Me
ALEC [Alexander Trilogy Book One]
ALEXANDER [Alexander Trilogy Book Two]
SACHA—THE WAY BACK
[Alexander Trilogy Book Three]
THE AVATAR SYNDROME
[Prequel to the Headless World]
HEADLESS WORLD
[Sequel to the Avatar Syndrome]
NOW—BEING AND BECOMING

Short stories
THE JEWEL AND OTHER SHORT STORIES
Sci-Fi Series 1
Sci-Fi Series 2
Cats & Dogs Series

Acknowledgements

My gratitude to
A.Guillaumont, H.-Ch. Puech, G. Quispel, W. Till and Yassah 'Abd
Al Masih who established and translated
the original Coptic text used in this book.

Also my thanks to the
Academic Publishers Brill of Leiden, The Netherlands,
for permission to reprint the English translation of
THE GOSPEL ACCORDING TO THOMAS
[Copyright © E.J. Brill 1959]

Dedicated to

James the righteous
for whose sake
heaven and earth came into being

CONTENTS

FOREWORD   9
Historical background

INTRODUCTION   11

GENERAL NOTES   13

COMMENTARY   15
The Gospel According to Thomas

BIBLIOGRAPHY   185

FOREWORD

In December 1945, an Arab peasant stumbled across an earth-enware container. He was poking around a mountain near a town called Nag Hammadi, in Upper Egypt. The mountain was honeycombed with numerous caves, many of which had been used for burial. Hoping that the earthenware jar might contain gold the peasant smashed it with his mallet. To his utter disappointment he discovered nothing more than some papers. Altogether he found 13 leather-bound papyrus volumes, which in turn contained 52 trac-tates, among them the *Gospel according to Thomas*. The Gospel contains 114 *logia*, sayings of Jesus, all reprinted here verbatim in bold print, with all the original translators' comments. Five Coptic and Hebrew scholars, all specialists in Gnosticism and primitive Christian literature, had provided the authoritative translation (first published in 1959), which I have used as the basis for my Com-mentary. Since their literary style approximates more the language of the King James Version of the Bible, I have chosen it over the later translation published in 1978 and 1988 as part of the *Nag Hammadi Library*. Though the choice of words between the two translations varies considerably, the essence of the teaching re-mains the same.

Before venturing any further, I wish to stress that my commentary is not directed at any person who is a satisfied member of any church, religious group or organization. If indeed this book will prove of use to anyone, than it will be to people whose hunger for esoteric knowledge has not been sated by the teaching of the group to which they at present belong. Writing the Commentary had been a process of self-discovery or, more accurately, a process of the discovery of Self. I had few sources to lean on, few if any learned dissertations to fall back on. With hardly any exceptions, the only reference I used frequently was the King James Version of the Bible.

I also do not claim to have provided exhaustive explanation of the 114 'sayings of Jesus', quoted in the pages that follow. Rather, the *logia* invoked certain ideas, which, at the time of writing, I felt compelled to put down.

*****

INTRODUCTION

**Whoever finds the explanation of these words
will not taste death.**
Logion 1. The Gospel According to Thomas.

When I read the words quoted above I had two choices: I could ignore them, or I could try and find out if indeed some enigmatic truth is hidden behind them. There followed a prolonged period of study. Years later I became convinced that nothing is hidden behind these portentous words. Nothing at all. The words mean exactly what they say. They are not a parable; they are a statement of fact coming from One who had, according to ensuing scriptures, proven their veracity.

From a scholarly point of view, I do not, nor did I at the time of writing, consider myself qualified to make doctrinaire pronouncements on the secrets contained in *The Gospel According to Thomas.* But even if I had such qualifications, I would have been reluctant to impose my conclusions on my neighbor. I might adversely affect the reader's peace of mind. I was stuck. I wanted to share my discovery, yet, in a way, I was afraid. After all, there are countless thousands of fully accredited professors, doctors of theology, divinity, theosophy, philosophy, and hosts of other equally

qualified people who busy themselves telling people how to interpret the Scriptures. But then I remembered Benjamin Hoff quoting
the teaching of Lao-tse and the ancient principles of Taoism. According to Mr. Hoff, Lao-tse affirms that: "Heaven... communicates
its deepest secrets to little children, animals, and *fools.*" I took a
deep breath—I might qualify after all! I found Lao-tse's statement
particularly reassuring, since what I really had to offer to my readers was a considered opinion that everyone must interpret the
Scriptures all by himself or herself.

That's right.

At the risk of sounding pompous, I confess that this is the
sum-total, the absolute summation, the deep conclusion that I have
reached after years of study. Could I be wrong? Of course. But
since practically all other methods aimed at the comprehension of
the Scriptures had been already tried, and the world appears to be
hardly better for it, I had relatively little to lose. If I am wrong, little will change. If, by any chance, I'd stumbled across something—
then this book offers the *Key to Immortality.*

As I was saying, I have relatively little to lose.

*****

GENERAL NOTES

As a resident of North America I chose to write my Commentary in the Canadian (or American) idiom while retaining the British spelling used by the translators in their English text (bold lettering). I have also retained their original punctuation, grammar and textual signs. My copy of the Gospel According to Thomas does not offer any explanations for these sings. Since, however, they appear to correspond to the signs used by the many translators of the Nag Hammadi Library [Revised Edition, James M. Robinson General Editor], I offer their abbreviated explanations of such.

[   ]   Square brackets indicate a lacuna in the manuscript with the translators' proposed reconstruction.

[...]   Indicates a lacuna where the text cannot be constructed, regardless of its length.

< >   Words within the pointed brackets indicate a correction of an apparent scribal omission or error.

(   )   Parentheses appear to indicate material supplied by the translators, presumably deemed necessary for the proper understanding of the original text.

*   I have added the asterisks as references to the translators' comments.

*****

THE GOSPEL ACCORDING TO THOMAS

COMMENTARY

1

These are the secret words which the Living Jesus spoke and Didymos Judas Thomas wrote.
1.   And He said: "Whoever finds the explanation of these words will not taste death."

Shall not taste death. What more can one expect? Is a promise, an assurance of immortality enough to make us listen? Enough to make us strive? Do we really want to live *that* long? Most of us associate the concept of immortality (or its apparent futility) with old age, creaky joints, feebleness of mind and body; certainly not with the *joie de vivre* promised elsewhere in the inspired *logia*.

What, then, of life and death? It may come as a shock to some, but this elusive promise of immortality has little to do with the aging process. In fact, it has nothing whatever to do with that which *we* call life. If we equate life with our physical body, with our physiological wellbeing, then, in the words of Jesus, we are either still, or already *dead*.[1] In fact it is as though we had never even been born.

Life referred to by Jesus is always and exclusively Spiritual Life. We must first be awakened to it not by some symbolic gesture of dipping ourselves in water or by having water sprinkled over our unsuspecting pates. [2]

The Life referred to by Jesus is, as with everything else He taught, a State of Consciousness. It is our awareness of who we are, of our heritage, of our birthright that ultimately leads to and results in Life Eternal. Those countless souls who expect that one day someone or Someone will come to this pale blue speck of dirt hanging on invisible strings on the periphery of a forgotten galaxy and set things in order... well, they will have a long wait. One might say eternal wait. Cycle after cycle of rebirth into a human form, years of walking around in circles, the wheel of Awagawan (the coming and going), the living dead... A fairly accurate description of *physical* evolution. An English scientist, James Burke, once

---

[1]   Matthew: 22 et al.

[2]   Such functions, as most other such rites, are only symbolic of the real meaning that lay behind their origin. The baptism administered to one whose consciousness is neither ready, nor might ever be ready in this present lifetime cannot be traced to any teaching of Jesus that I know of. Most Christian churches claim nowadays that the baptismal rites are to cleanse an innocent child of its inherited sin. Yet Jesus refers to children as to souls by far nearest to Heaven, to the Heavenly Father. But even if the youngsters did bear some iniquity imposed on them by their forefathers, it is hard to imagine how a perfunctory ablution might serve to absolve them of some such stigma.

Originally, the so-called *seed-karma* may have been the antecedent that led John the Baptist to introduce baptism. The seed-karma is said to precede the first incarnation. Alternatively, an equally ancient belief that soul leaves the human body through the thousand-petalled lotus chakra, supposedly situated at one's crown, may have been at the root, or rather the head of the custom of administering water (perhaps originally oils) to the top of one's head. It may have symbolized the will to maintain the bones in one's cranium in a flexible condition, thus aiding the soul in its desire to free itself of its earthly prison.

described the rate of evolution as "somewhere between dead slow and dead slow."

The purpose of physical universe is to demonstrate the results of positive or negative thinking or attitudes by employing the concept of dualism. Black and white, up and down, red and green, loud and silent, music and noise, harmony and discord, movement and stillness. Physical life is movement. It is the manifestation of the Stillness Within. Spirit is static. It is beyond time and space. Physical life, indeed physical universe, the countless planets, stars, galaxies, are all entirely dependent on movement. On transience. That which moves has a beginning and an end. That which is static is Eternal. Unchangeable. Like Spirit. Like the Father in Heaven. Like the Heaven within us.

Whoever finds the explanation of these words shall not taste death. Whoever finds the explanation of these words will have found the true Life, the immortal, immovable center of stillness within oneself that cannot be influenced by *any* external factors. A stillness that is completely independent of any physical manifestations; which cannot be injured, harmed or abused by anyone, nor anything, in the physical universe. It is the center from which emanates Peace *which passeth all understanding.*[3]

He, who finds the explanation of these words shall have found Life eternal, shall have discovered his or her true Self. They who identify with the true Self as the sole Essence of their Being simply say: I and my Father are One.

***

---

[3]   Philippians 4:7

2

Jesus said: Let him who seeks, not cease seeking until he finds, and when he finds, he will be troubled, and when he has been troubled, he will marvel and he will reign over the All.

This is an accurate, and apparently universal, description of the road to self-discovery; perhaps more accurately described as the discovery of self. When first breaching the intangible chasm that separates the physical from the Higher Consciousness, the sense of 'being troubled' is overwhelming. One expects heavens to rend asunder and a sword of divine lightening to strike one for daring to cross this forbidden threshold.

Later, having survived this event, one marvels and the sense of wonder lingers on.

The final phase, the "reign over the All" is a more gradual process—that of dawning realization. It is a gradual awakening to one's true nature. It comes as a shock, often a series of traumatic experiences, to all that have been brought up in no matter what religion. Though one should add that seldom the realization of Self comes to those who are steeped in orthodox teachings. As it had been said: "one does not pour new wine into old skins", or, even more strongly: *"I make ALL things ne"*[4]. In order to accept the new, one must let go of the old. We must let go of the old concepts,

---

[4]   Revelation 21:5 (my capitalizing)

19

old ideas, old dogmas, old beliefs.[5] We must let go of one's past. All of it. In order to become free. Then... then New Heaven and New Earth can finally come into being in our consciousness. The experience can be quite scary. On the other hand, no one said it would be easy.

Heaven is for the daring, the brave.

***

---

[5]   It may be of some interest that the loudest advocates of traditions are the governments (particularly military juntas) and churches. It seems that those who wish to control consciousness of other people have most to lose by letting go of the past. Traditions, be they nationalistic, religious or even cultural give us a pleasant sense of security and emotional belonging, but they are apt to anchor us in our past.

3

Jesus said: If those who lead you say to you: "See, the Kingdom is in heaven", then the birds of the heaven will precede you. If they say to you: "It is in the sea," then the fish will precede you. But the Kingdom is within you and it is without you. If you (will) know yourselves, then you will be known and will know that you are the sons of the Living Father. But if you do not know yourselves, then you are in poverty and you are poverty.

The Kingdom was, is and always will be a STATE OF CONSCIOUSNESS. As such, it cannot be but: 'within you'. One wonders why, after so many years, various religions still choose to ignore these particular assertions of Jesus. Assertions repeated almost *ad nauseam* in so many statements attributed to Him. Heaven is WITHIN you. Neither after death, nor above nor below. It is neither before nor after. It is neither reward nor punishment. It is a state of consciousness that comes—in time—to all that seek. We have this assurance in the previous *logion*. We have it repeated in the four gospels regardless of the degree of enlightenment of the translator. It shines as brightly in the King James Version of the Bible as in the Vulgate.[6] It is stated repeatedly in all the Scriptures yet, apparently, accepted by few of the so-called 'believers'. Many religious leaders will tell us that if we are good we shall be saved. That we shall "go" to heaven. Quite the contrary! Once we are saved we might begin to understand what it is to be good. You or I might be 'good' because we are saved—we are certainly not saved

---

[6]   The Vulgate is the Latin version of the Bible prepared by St. Jerome (c.347 - 419?), which is recognized by the Roman Catholic Church as the Authorized Version.

because we are 'good'. Jesus assures us that *only* God is good.[7]

The second paragraph carries some of the marvel referred to in previous *logion*. *If you will know yourselves, then you will be known and will know that you are the sons of the Living Father.* Jesus is saying that you must know YOURSELF. That you must know who YOU really are, your OWN true nature. Not that you or I are sinners, nor that from the moment of birth, a tiny baby, we must strain under the millstone of the "original sin".[8] He assures us that when we finally know ourselves, *we shall know that we are sons of the Living Father.* And when we do, most incredible things begin to happen within our consciousness. We begin to wonder, again with that marvel mentioned above, just who is this mysterious Father. This *Living Father.* In time we find out. And then our realization of truth deepens. And finally, when we are ready, *we shall rein over the All.*

But wait! We are told that "the Kingdom of heaven is within you and *without* you." Isn't it obvious? Everything, absolutely EVERYTHING that our senses, our imagination, our emotions or our minds can touch is a State of Consciousness. The true reality. The TRUTH. It cannot be otherwise. The trick is to identify oneself with the cause and not with the result. The cause is always the Spirit. The Higher Self. The Father in Heaven. It is that which precedes our minds or our mental perception. The physical is the ultimate result. The end product of a creative process.

***

---

[7]   In Matthew 19:16-17 Jesus remonstrates with a follower saying: *"Why callest thou me good? There is none good but one, that is, God..."*

[8]   In my essay entitled *"Pleasure"* [BEYOND RELIGION I, Inhousepress 1997, 2001, 2002] I make the following comment: *"The original sin had been invented by St. Augustine in the 4th century AD. The concept does not exist in the Christian Bible, nor in the Jewish Torah. And so says Mathew Fox, a Catholic priest".*

4

Jesus said: The man old in days will not hesitate to ask a little child of seven days about the place of Life, and he will live. For many who are first shall become last and they shall become as a single one.

This is a little more complicated. At least, at first sight. To understand this *logion* fully we would best look up prophet Isaiah. He tells us: "For unto us a *child* is born, unto us a son is given: and the government shall be upon his shoulder: and his name shall be called Wonderful, Counsellor, The mighty God, The everlasting Father, The Prince of Peace."[9] A *child of seven days*. In all scriptural writings the number seven symbolizes perfection, a state of completion. The world was completed in six days and on the *seventh* day God ended his work, which he had made.[10] The work was done; the state of completion, of wholeness has been achieved.

Isaiah was talking, of course, about the new State of Consciousness, which is (shall be) born in peoples' awareness. After long struggles, people that walked in darkness have seen a great light: they that dwell in the land of the shadow of death, upon them hath the light shined.[11] Light, in the Bible, invariably symbolizes divine knowledge, or more accurately, the Source of Divine Knowledge.

Now we return to the *logion*.

A man old in days is you and I. We are old in days. Contrary to the Spirit, we are held in a matrix of time. We are old, perhaps tired. And then, often suddenly, we become aware of a new state of

---

9   Isaiah 9:6 et seq. (my emphasis)

10   Genesis 2:2

11   Isaiah 9:2

consciousness within us. Note: always *within* us. A State of Consciousness so new that we refer to It as a child. A child of seven days. A perfect child. We do not hesitate to ask this child, this new state of awareness about *the place of Life*. We already know the answer. We have discovered the Stillness. A state of immortality. Little wonder that we shall Live. We came into this world first, but now we are more than willing to give reins of our kingdom, our state of consciousness, to this new found awareness. To this Child. We are willing to become second fiddle, to become last. To become *as a single one* with That which is born within us.

Eventual realization of this singularity is later exemplified in the statement "I and (my) father are one."[12]

***

---

[12] John 10:30

5

Jesus said: Know what* is in thy sight, and what is hidden from thee will be revealed to thee. For there is nothing hidden which will not be manifest.
   *(Translators' comment) or: **"him who"**.

   There are no secrets. There never were. Jesus spoke in parables not to confuse us only to help us. But it hadn't been easy to
address people who could neither read nor write. People whose
main concern had been to 'make the ends meet,' to feed their children, to assure a roof over their heads. People refused to believe
that That which is within them is greater than that which is without.
That He who created the Within also created the without. By observing the result we learn about the Cause. And the result is, of
course, the universe around us. God, the Creative Force, is manifest
in all that we can see, smell, taste, hear, feel, imagine, grasp with
our minds. It is an illusion God creates for us to help us in our purpose.
   The *logion* further suggests that the Truth is right in front of
our noses, that it is immediately apparent; that we can discover this
sublime Reality in our immediate vicinity—without resorting to
profound philosophical or theological dissertations.
   The translators suggest an alternate meaning to this *legion*.
Know *him* who is in thy sight. If we accept this meaning, than the
revelation is even more profound. It means that once we discover
Him who is within us, within our sight, all else shall be revealed to
us. A tempting offer indeed!

***

6

His disciples asked Him, they said to Him: Wouldst thou* that we fast and how should we pray (and) should we give alms, and what diet should we observe? Jesus said: Do not lie; and do not do what you hate, for all things are manifest before Heaven.* For there is nothing hidden that shall not be revealed and there is nothing covered that shall remain without being uncovered.

(*Translators' comments) **"How wouldst thou"**

(*Translators' comments) **"Heaven": perhaps** originally **"the Truth"**.

How severely the divine patience is tested by the well meaning but still oh... so ignorant followers. Jesus tells them of the Divine Consciousness, of the Kingdom NOT of this world, of the Life within, and they, His very own disciples, ask Him about their diet! Jesus ignores them. *Do not lie. Do not do what you hate.* Why? Because when you do, you place other things before the Truth. Truth must come first. Always. The Spiritual Truth. Because whatever you do is known to your own Higher Self. Because by lying you separate yourself from your Higher Self. From the Child within waiting to be born.

For there is nothing that you do that is or can be hidden from your *own* true Self. Nothing. After all, though you do not know it yet, the Child is perfect. Complete. It already knows that you and It (He) are one. And the Child is Wonderful, The Prince of Peace. How could It possibly do something It hates? How can you?

***

7

Jesus said: Blessed is the lion which the man eats and the lion will become man; and cursed is the man whom the lion eats and the lion will become man.*
(*Transl. comment) **"the man will become lion."**

Here we go back to Biblical symbolism. Lion symbolizes a known, if considerable difficulty to be overcome (as against a dragon which lurks deep in our subconscious).[13] Man is the expression, a manifestation of his internal life. Of his inner struggles. Whatever we overcome that we become. The difficulty becomes a victory. We win battles. We develop faith in our own power. We begin to identify with that within us, which is invincible. Almighty. We become Princes. Then Kings. Ultimately we *will rein over the all* (*logion 2*).

Whatever overcomes us, however, also becomes manifest in our mortal nature. Blessed is the man who overcomes great difficulties. He must first become aware of them. He must face them and win. All difficulties are placed in our path for one single purpose: to bring us closer to our true Self. To spiritualize our consciousness.

***

---

[13]   Kapuscinski,   Stanislaw: DICTIONARY   OF   BIBLICAL SYMBOLISM

8

And He said: The Man is like a wise fisherman who cast his net into the sea full of small fish; among them he found a large (and) good fish, that wise fisherman, he threw all the small fish down into the sea, he chose the large fish without regret. Whoever has ears to hear let him hear.

There are many roads leading to Heaven. In fact, as many as there are people in the world. A man casts his net; he tries to cast as broad, as wide reaching a net as he can, to study as many alternative routes as possible. He studies philosophies of the ancients, religions reaching back to the dawn of humanity, religions which originated a mere 2000 years ago, New Age trends and avocations. He studies sciences, mathematics, arts, music. Many, many small fish. At least a wise man has initiated his search. But in his inexperience he searches everywhere. It makes one wonder at the words of the psalmist: *"If I ascend up into heaven, thou art there: if I make my bed in hell, behold, thou art there."*[14] Searching for that which is everywhere yet nowhere. For that which is intangible, which does and can exist only on one's consciousness.

It is like not seeing the trees for the forest.

Jesus makes it easy for us all. He states and repeats again and again: "Heaven is within you." True, it is manifested also without you, but why search far and wide when that which you search for is right here? It cannot be closer to you than your own heart. Your soul.

---

[14]   Psalm 139:8

When the wise fisherman finds this one, singular wonderful prize, this good large fish, this idea-concept, he throws all other fish (ideas-concepts-speculations) away. He keeps only the one. The one that cannot get away. The one within.

***

9

Jesus said: See, the sower went out, he filled his hand he threw. Some (seeds) fell on the road; the birds came, they gathered them. Others fell on the rock and did not strike root in the earth and did not produce ears. And others fell on the thorns; they choked the seed and the worm ate them. And others fell on the good earth; and it brought forth good fruit; it bore sixty per measure and on hundred twenty per measure.

This *logion* is very similar to the previous one. Jesus found it necessary to describe the same philosophy, the same truth in many different ways in the hope that at least one of them might fall on good earth and bear fruit. The teaching is so simple a child has no problems understanding it.

I am reminded of a statement made by the late Edgar Cayce, the man known as the sleeping prophet. Once asked which version of the Bible is the nearest to the true meaning of the Old and New Testaments, he replied (inter alia) "*....remember that the whole gospel of Jesus Christ is, 'Thou shalt love the Lord thy God with all thy mind, thy heart and thy body; and thy neighbor as thyself. Do this and thou shalt have eternal life.' The rest of the book is trying to describe that.*"[15]

How true.

We learn by trial and error.

We are like the sower who casts his seed on untested soil. We struggle. All Jesus was trying to do was to make life easier for us. "Come to me, all ye that labour and are heavy laden and I will

---

[15]   THE EDGAR CAYCE READER #2.

give you rest."[16]   Tired of trying, of abortive efforts. Of endless
failures. Apparently it does not have to be so difficult. Just: "love
My presence within you as well as My presence all around you..."
He seems to be saying. The rest will fall into place. All by itself.
     Seems easy.

***

---

[16]   Matthew 11:28

10

Jesus said: I have cast* fire upon the world, and see, I guard it until it (the world) is afire.

*(Transl. comments): **"I have cast"** read probably: **"I have come to cast"**

In the scriptures, fire always symbolizes cleansing. The cleansing of our consciousness. Ridding our minds of the dross accumulated over years of abortive efforts. Ridding us of the dross forced into our minds by the countless religions over countless thousands of years. The admonition is to Know Thyself. Not to know your local church or your local religious leader. If it or he helps you towards the attainment of the knowledge of Self, all's well and good. If he forces upon you his or her own 'ideas'—run. You can listen to his or her words or to the words of Jesus. It's your choice.

This is *not* an anti-religious dissertation. I firmly believe that (almost) every religion (church, sect) is started in the name of the highest possible ethical standards. I also believe that for some, it is better to practice their religion for an hour on a Sunday, than not to reflect on their inner potential at all. Unfortunately after a new sect comes into being, in order to survive, it must grow. As the organization grows, it gains power. It becomes a kingdom. Earthly kingdom. It starts with a cleansing process, with fire, but soon it drowns in its own accumulated dross. It begins to control people. It takes from people a divine gift: the gift of free will.

Then, in a show of intuitive rebellion, yet a new religion

comes. And the cycle repeats itself.[17] It may surprise many that Jesus had never started a religion. In fact He had nothing good to say about any religion of His time. He invariably advocated direct contact with the divinity within us. Never through an intermediary.

The fire is not a punishment. He who is the embodiment of love does not punish. Fire is sustained in this world, i.e.: in this, the physical state of consciousness, until this state becomes cleansed. Purified. Ultimately—made whole.

***

---

[17]   In the first World Council of Churches (1948) Meeting, more than 200 churches, (sects, denominations) met in an attempt to resolve their differences. Needless to say, no unification has been achieved. And those were only Christian denominations. How may other are there? How many came into being since 1948?

11

Jesus said: This heaven shall pass away and the one above it shall pass away, and the dead are not alive and the living shall not die. In the days when you devoured the dead, you made it alive; and you come into light, what will you do? On the day when you were one, you became two. But when you have become two, what will you do?

This heaven, and all heavens, is progressively higher and higher state of consciousness. Higher state of awareness. There is no limit to the evolution of consciousness. There can be no limit to the expansion of the concept of God. How long does it take to encompass Infinity?

The dead are the *spiritually* dead. Those who are not as yet aware of their Divine heritage. The living cannot die because they identify with that which is Immortal within them. Their consciousness is no longer centered on the material, transient world. It is completely assimilated into that which is indestructible. They are in this world but not of this world.

To devour the dead means to overcome that, which is spiritually dead, i.e.: our lower nature, our physical or material or transient state of consciousness. By overcoming it we rise to a higher level.

We become alive.

And here Jesus indulges in a very rare moment of philosophy. He says: When *you come into light, what will you do?* In the Scriptures, Light is spiritual knowledge. Always. We might as well agree here, once and for all, that Jesus taught only, exclusively, inconvertibly *spiritual* Truth. What you did with your physical body was of very little interest to Him. That which was physical or material was dead to Him. It was the result, whereas Jesus had been concerned only with the Cause. Life meant always Spiritual Life. The soul, the consciousness the Inner Self was all that He'd ever cared about.

When Jesus muses: what *will you do?* He muses about your and mine, perhaps anyone's spiritual future. Many have mused before Him, many since. There are religions, which insist that when we die, we shall go to heaven (assuming we earned it, of course). There, they say, we shall be eternally happy, apparently sitting on the side or in front or next to an exalted throne, upon which a god will sit. The god's face will be old and kindly, with just enough severity radiating from his splendid features to scare the laggards into behaving themselves. Others, particularly the TV evangelists, admonish us to hurry up! The Millennium is coming, they say. For a thousand years you will be happy! Whether you like it or not!

   ...you come into light, what will you do?
   As previously stated, there is no end to God, there is no end to the expansion of our consciousness. That which is within us is infinite. That which is within you is You. The real You. So... *what will you do?* Now you have come into the light. You have acquired some knowledge. In the Scriptures Jacob symbolizes such a condition. Jacob is a soul, a state of consciousness, finally aware of its spiritual nature, but not yet aware of its divine origin. The first step.
   ...what will you do?
   On the day you were born into this physical world, you were One. You were a single spark of God, a singular, individual drop of the Infinite Ocean of Divine Love. And you became two. You became the proud possessor of a dual nature. Your Higher Self remained within the temple of your heart, and your lower nature, the personality, came into being of its own.

   Well, at this stage some continue on the path, others take a rest, still others take a side road leading to nowhere. Not through ill will. Perhaps they are afraid. The promises do seem too good to be true!
   It is up to us. You and me.
   Always.
   Yet the strange thing is that it is not the destination that really

matters so much. The destination is an ever-receding horizon, ever-unfolding wonder, marvel, miraculous existence. What really matters then—is the trip. The journey. The experience. So please, please enjoy it. As so many wise men will tell you, you only have one life to live. Even if it is eternal.

There is no purpose to life but life itself.

The process of becoming.

***

12

The disciples said to Jesus: We know that thou wilt go away from us. Who is it who shall be great over us? Jesus said to them: Wherever you have come, you will go to James the righteous for whose sake heaven and earth came into being.

It must have been truly heartbreaking. After all these years, after all the lessons, direct as well as in the form of countless parables, after shedding constant example... what a question! *Who is it who shall be great over us?*

Why is it that people have such inherent need to be slaves? If not priests then psychiatrists, if not kings then politicians, if not nobility then demagogues who usurped power by force. Recent history of Central America is such a painful example of this human weakness. No sooner had one regime been disposed of by a gallant junta, always in the name and at the cost of the oppressed, when the new regime became the oppressors. *Da capo al fine.* A *rondo capriccioso.* Like some strange, capricious dance of a snake swallowing its own tail. In a sense, we all seem to be doing the same thing at our own, individual level. *Who shall be great over us?*

James. James the righteous. *Wherever you have come.* Whatever state of consciousness you have reached, go to James the righteous. After all, it is for him that this marvelous dualistic system came into being. The heaven and the earth. The two states of consciousness, which immediately show the results of your thoughts, decisions, actions. But most of all, as I mentioned in my comments on the previous *logion*, it is an eternal process of becoming.

James, in the New Testament, is the English equivalent of Jacob. That's right. The man who is already aware of his spiritual nature. Not any more, as yet, but he is already aware of it. That's all. Go to him. He is the righteous. He is thinking right. He has already started. Until this first spark of enlightenment he was dead. Go to him.

If any of what you are reading here makes any sense to you, then he is you. Not if you agree with it all, only if it makes any sense. Go into your own heart.

***

13

Jesus said to his disciples: Make a comparison to Me and tell Me whom I am like. Simon Peter said to Him: Thou art like a righteous angel. Matthew said to Him: Thou art like a wise man of understanding. Thomas said to Him: Master, my mouth will not at all be capable of saying whom Thou art like. Jesus said: I am not thy Master, because thou hast drunk, thou hast become drunk from the bubbling spring which I have measured* out. And He took him, He withdrew, He spoke three words to him. Now when Thomas came to his companions, they asked him: What did Jesus say to thee? Thomas said to them: If I tell you one of the words which He said to me, you will take up stones and throw at me; and fire will come from the stones and burn you up.

*(Transl. comment) **"measured"**; perhaps: **"dug"**.

Jesus said: I am not your Master.
What then? The Lord? The Son of God? God Itself?
"I am not your master. You have been born free. You came into being as a Divine Spark of Infinite Consciousness. You are an immortal Entity. Many will try to enslave you by opposing themselves between you and your and my Father, but not I."
You have drunk from the bubbling spring. You have drunk of the knowledge of the eternal, inexhaustible spring of Life. Perhaps too fast, too much. Perhaps you identify the man at the Spring with the Spring Itself. Look closer. The Spring is also within you. Bubbling. Waiting for you, offering you all you can drink. Look..."

One can only wonder at what ghastly secret Jesus must have told Thomas. What terrible knowledge must have been imparted to his disciple, the consequences of which would result in instant stoning. Instant death. In the days of Jesus only one such transgression called for such frightful punishment. Blasphemy. Blasphemy against the unspeakable name of god. The Hebrew god. The god of vengeance. And the secret? I suspect that Jesus told Thomas the truth about His divine origin. Not only His own but also Thomas's. Such realization would have been traumatic. To most people it is equally as traumatic today. Yet it is the Psalmist who had first spoken the three unspeakable words: *Ye are gods.*[18] Sons, daughters, of God.

To other disciples, two thousand years ago, such an assertion would have sounded like blasphemy. Today not many have the inner strength to face a mirror, look deep into their own eyes, search out the mysterious Self within the depth of their own intent unwavering gaze and say: Be *still, and know that I am God.*[19] You don't think so? Try it.

Later, it is for enunciating this very Truth that Jesus had been crucified. Perhaps when He took Thomas aside he tried not to think about the rest of the Psalmist's promise. *Ye are gods...*said David, whose name became the symbol of Divine Love, *Ye are gods... but ye shall die like men, and fall like one of the princes.*

We all know the Psalmist was right about the second part of his promise. How about the first?

***

---

[18]   Psalm 82:6

[19]   Psalm 46:10

14

Jesus said to them: If you fast, you will beget sin for yourselves, and if you pray, you will be condemned, and if you give alms, you will do evil to your spirits. And if you go into any land and wander in the regions, if they receive you, eat what they set before you, heal the sick among them. For what goes into your mouth will not defile you, but what comes out of your mouth, that is what will defile you.

Fast from what. Meat, vegetables, fruit?

We are told not to abstain from Spiritual Food. Not to refrain from raising our consciousness to admit Light, to admit spiritual knowledge. If we do, we shall beget sin for ourselves. In the New Testament, the Greek word *hamartia* or *hamartano*, translated as *sin*, originates from the sport or archery. Literal meaning is *missing the mark*. Missing the heart of the problem. Fasting of any nature is missing the point. When we concentrate on abstaining from 'physical' food, we are preoccupied with our bodies; not with our spiritual nature. What we eat is, we are told, of little or no consequence. What we feed our souls—is.

Again we are reminded that Jesus was neither a dietician nor a doctor of medicine. Jesus healed the state of mind, or more accurately, the state of consciousness that hindered the flow of the creative energy or the life force to which Jesus referred as Spirit. He regarded human body as a spiritual idea, and *spiritual* ideas, by definition, are perfect even as the Spirit is perfect. When left alone, our physical body functions as the Spirit would have it function. However... we have been granted free will.[20] From the moment we

---

[20]   We must acknowledge that anything that is perfect is, by definition, in a state of stasis. You can't improve on perfection. The gift of free will allows us to experiment, to rise to ever-new heights, to reach and

learn to walk, we assert our puny egos by setting our will in direct opposition to the Spirit. Every teenager does this towards his or her parents. When they (we) grow up, they (we) do it in relation to our Higher Self. Edgar Cayce once said that there is only one sin, and that is selfishness. The little self. Ego. Ego (personality) is what keeps us apart from the Whole. Individuality (from Latin *individuus* or indivisible) is what draws us together.

Perhaps it should be mentioned that physical cures attributed to Jesus had been the by-products of His healing influence, not its purpose. Jesus knew well that all things physical are transient. A cure of a physical abrasion, inadequacy, disease, would never be permanent. We are gods, but we shall die like men. No matter what the 'cure'.

And now we come to the more difficult part: *...and if you pray you will be condemned.* A strange statement. How can prayer bring about condemnation? Thomas in his ardent effort to jot down all that Jesus had said must have done so in somewhat of a hurry. This *logion* is quite obviously a continuation of *logion 6*, in which Jesus apparently chose to ignore the question. Here He answers it fully. To understand the answer, however, we must backtrack a little and study the Biblical, or Scriptural language. When the scribes of the Old Testament wanted to describe 'spiritual' prayer, they referred to it as going towards, or up to, a mountain. Or at least a hill. The higher the better. By this metaphor the scribes tried to imply the raising of one's consciousness. Moses, Joshua, Isaiah, Amos, all the prophets, indeed Jesus Himself went up the mountain. They each raised their individual consciousness. They aspired to direct contact with their Higher Self. With the Father in Heaven. That was *real* prayer.

What the Jews meant by prayer, however, was quite different. When they 'prayed' they asked for 'things' concerning their physical wellbeing. For things which would make their physical

---

cross new horizons. In the process we are in danger of missing the mark (sin), and an influx of the life-force (intelligence) is necessary to set us on the straight and narrow. It may be of interest to readers that if it weren't for mutations, evolution would grind to a stop. Yet mutations are little more than natures 'mistakes' (sins) or departures from an established path.

lives more comfortable, all too often at the expense of their neighbor. Now this is the type of prayer that Jesus said would condemn you. Why? First—because it deviates our efforts from the edification of our individual souls. Secondly—because it presupposes that our Higher Self, our Father, doesn't know much better than we what is good for us. *Take therefore no thought for the morrow: for the morrow shall take thought for the things of itself.*[21]

...*and if you give alms, you will do evil to your spirits.* This seems the most difficult, almost blood curling statement. You give alms, and for your generosity you do evil to your sprit. But is it so absurd? Let us look at the previous statement. God, Spirit, knows exactly what It is doing. It places all people in circumstances that are absolutely mandatory for them to raise their consciousness. It carefully lays out circumstances in which those lucky souls can raise themselves above their present level. It may have taken many years, perhaps lifetimes, to set up just the right conditions. The Spirit, or more precisely the Law of the Spirit, is *very* exacting. And then, a presumptuous do-gooder comes along and changes the exigent circumstances. He, or she, gives *material* alms and thus drags the delinquent soul back to the physical awareness.

It is very difficult to be blessed and not to share one's blessings. But we must be very careful. We must always give, but give with tremendous discrimination. I do not mean that we should spend hours on assessing who is the most needy. A rich-man is probably much poorer spiritually than one sleeping on a park bench. If we offer the wrong gift at the wrong time to the wrong person, we shall bear the resultant karma; which simply means that, as with everything else, we shall bear the consequences of our actions. We shall be responsible. We must never loose sight that the sole purpose of our earthly life is to advance our learning process—it is a search for our Kingdom.[22]

And by the way. If we should have given and didn't, we are quite as guilty. We miss the mark (i.e.: we 'sin') just as badly, as if we gave the right thing to the wrong person. It is not easy being

---

[21]   Matthew 6:34

[22]   Incidentally. When we do, we discover to our amazement that the Kingdom is already here.

gods.

Even apprentice gods.

The admonition to *eat what they set before you* carries a dual meaning. The first meaning is directed at the Jews steeped in Hebrew traditions.[23] It is intended to set them free from outdated regulations. Jesus says that 'physically' they (we) may eat with no regard to the Jewish laws controlling the preparation of food. Such laws were of vital importance when the Jews had been wondering the desert (spiritual desert), when the level of their mental and spiritual development were such that the physical awareness constituted the dominant aspect of their consciousness. But now Light came into the world, and Light is knowledge. Comestibles are no longer of paramount importance. It is the spiritual food that matters. Thus we come to the second, the deeper meaning of the admonition.

We often hear the expression that we are what we eat. Well, according to Jesus, we are not. At best, we are what we think, although more precisely we are what we *believe* we are. Thoughts are things. If we control our thoughts, the physical body will take care of itself. Our thoughts come out of our mouths as words, as ideas. We must control them lest they defile us.

***

---

[23]   Few of us seem to realize that Jesus was first and foremost an iconoclast. In spite of this, Christians, as a rule, are enamoured with traditions of every imaginable sort.

15

Jesus said: When you see Him who was not born of woman, prostrate yourselves upon your face and adore Him: He is your Father.

We are all born of a woman. We are physical beings. At least—we think we are. Jesus disputes that. He claims that we are spiritual beings finding a temporary abode in physical envelopes of flesh. Not bodies possessed of a soul, but Soul expressing Itself through a body. A very fundamental difference. It is a question of a point of view.

Throughout the ages mystics have advocated contemplation as a prerequisite to spiritual growth. Those who practice contemplation, who climb the highest mountain—as the Biblical prophets would call it—can expect, in time, to behold that which cannot be seen with physical eyes. It cannot be seen, measured, weighed or dissected in a laboratory. We can behold, perhaps experience, perhaps sense with supra-natural senses, the essence of our true being. We sense that which is not born of a woman. We sense that which is born of Spirit. That is our Father. It is the Center of our Consciousness, our indivisible conjunction with the Infinite. It is that within us which is immortal, indestructible. It is the Source of our existence. Some experience this Essence as Light, some as heavenly music, some personify It into a quasi-human form. However It chooses to reveal Itself to us, we all fall on our faces and adore It.

The trick is to grasp that instant of eternity. *Behold, I come as a thief,*[24] in the night, unexpectedly. If we do not cease the mo-

---

[24]   Revelation 16:15

ment... it might pass. We must live in a state of preparedness. In constant vigilance. Within an atmosphere of attentive expectation. To recognize Spirit we must live like spiritual beings. No one said it would be easy.

***

16

Jesus said: Men possibly think that I have come to throw peace upon the world and they do not know that I have come to throw divisions upon the earth, fire, sword, war. For there shall be five in a house: three shall be against two and two against three, the father against the son and the son against the father, and they will stand as solitaries.

Those of us who still expect that Jesus shall return in full glory as the *ex cathedra* ruler of the world and that He shall declare universal or at least global peace for a thousand years, well, they better read this *logion* again. It is evident that Jesus found it necessary to repeat and redefine *ad nauseam* that His interest, His philosophy, His all-consuming attention is centered on, and directed exclusively towards, the soul, and not the body. Bodies are dispensable, exchangeable, reducible into dust from whence they came. Why is it that so many of us cannot understand this simple truth? Why is this truth as difficult to understand today, as it must have been some 2000 years ago?

...ye are of this world: I am not of this world.[25]

"What you see with your eyes is maya. An illusion. What you perceive with your senses is a feeble mirage of the splendor within. The true reality, the only reality, is Spirit," He seems to be saying. Again and again.

...I am not of this world,[26] Jesus declares repeatedly. *My Kingdom is not of this world...* [27] He repeats on and on and on...

---

[25]   John 8:23

[26]   John 17:16

[27]   John 18:36

Whatever He taught seems to have fallen, and continues to fall, on dead ears. *WHY DO YE NOT UNDERSTAND MY SPEECH?*[28] He asks another time. Why can't you understand me?

Why can't we?

It is well evident that Jesus was willing to do everything in his power to open the eyes and the ears of His people. Under the circumstances, He was often forced to take chances with being misunderstood. His words almost invariable carry a double meaning. The interpretations will depend upon the level to which the listener's consciousness has unfolded. The first is the so-called 'fundamental', (or, *à la lettre,* verbatim, or literal) interpretation. It might be said that it deals with the letter rather than the spirit of the law. In this *logion,* the fundamental meaning that fire, sword, wars, even as the breakdown of families... all such horrors are, comparatively speaking, of no consequence. None of these *really* matter. What truly matters is spiritual awakening. If it takes strife, fire, sword, war—so be it. No millennium of peace and lackadaisical boredom.

Only be careful! Love thy neighbor. The fire is cleansing, the swords cuts us off from redundant appurtenances, the wars... the wars we fight daily with our egos. The families? The mind-sets resulting from years of abortive repetition. Whole families of errors. And thus we come to the deeper, the spiritual meaning.

The *five in a house* are our five principle states of consciousness, our inner and outer 'bodies': the spiritual, mental, causal, emotional and physical.[29] Elsewhere in the Scriptures such wars, such battles are compared to earthquakes: *...and there was a great earthquake, such as was not since men were upon the earth, so mighty an earthquake, and so great.*[30] These earthquakes, even as the wars, take place within our consciousness. We must win by

---

[28]   John 8:43

[29]   A 'house,' even as a town, city, tent, village or any other spatial constraint wherein one resides for any length of time invariably symbolizes various states of consciousness. For more information refer to DICTIONARY OF BIBLICAL SYMBOLISM by the author.

[30]   Revelation 16:18

loosing attachment to the nonessentials. When the Spirit com-
mands, we must be ready to give up every single old, cozy, comfortable, established idea. *Behold, I make all thing new.*[31] He certainly did. This is the spiritual meaning. We must never lose sight
that Jesus taught *only* spiritual knowledge. The Spirit is the only
reality, the only truth He recognized. He left unto Caesar things
that are Caesar's.[32] He left earthly matters to those who were interested in them.

He wasn't.

Should we be?

***

---

[31]   Revelation 21:5
[32]   Matthew 22:21, Mark 12:17, Luke 20:25, paraphrase.

17

Jesus said: I will give you what eye has not seen and what ear has not heard and what hand has not touched and (what) has not arisen in the heart of man.

The gifts of Spirit are always individual. Every one of us is a unique, un-repeatable expression of the sum total of all that we have accumulated over countless lives (embodiments) of our existence.[33] There are no two blades of grass that match each other exactly, let alone two human beings. That much we know.

What Jesus is referring to here is the uniqueness of our inner states of consciousness. We each express a condition of Spirit that cannot be repeated. Neither now nor ever in time. What Jesus had been teaching his disciples was to examine, to see and hear that which is within them. To see what no eye has seen, what no ear has heard, what no hand has touched. He was teaching them to look inwards, to get to know themselves. To do that, a new consciousness must arise in the heart of man. In our hearts.

***

---

[33] Spiritually we have but one life—with neither beginning nor end.

18

The disciples said to Jesus: Tell us how our end will be. Jesus said: Have you then discovered the beginning so that you inquire about the end? For where the beginning is, there shall be the end. Blessed is he who shall stand at the beginning, and he shall know the end and he shall not taste death.

The beginning is our original place. Heaven. A reality of infinite potential.

A Virtual Reality.

We embarked on a great, great journey. We learn, we study, we seek, knock... We arrive back were we had started. The original place. Heaven. In some ways, we've never left. Only now we are of some use. We paid our dues. We have learned. He who arrives there shall not taste death. He is no longer able to loose touch with his true Self. He and his Higher Self are One.

He has achieved immortality.

***

19

Jesus said: Blessed is he who was before he came into being. If you become disciples to Me and hear My words, these stones will minister to you. For you have five trees in Paradise, which are unmoved in summer or in winter and their leaves do not fall. Whoever knows them will not taste death.

To convey His message Jesus found it necessary to repeat the same truth in a thousand different ways. Sometimes changing the words, just slightly, in the hope that a new angle, a new slant would break through the built up barriers of the listeners' mind-set. It seems ironic that even such constant repetition did not assure Him of being understood. Neither by His nor by our contemporaries.

Once again, as in *logion 18*, He refers to the pre-birth condition. To the state the soul is in just prior to entering or assuming a physical body. Until this instant of eternity the soul is free.[34] It is beyond time and space. It is in Paradise. Furthermore when in this high state of consciousness, *these stones will minister to you*. In this state of consciousness, we (shall) have total command over all aspects of physical reality.

And here Jesus casts a new light on the nature of Paradise. Many teachers of truth assert that as we enter Paradise, we must

---

[34]   In the biblical idiom, 'soul' is usually a translation of Hebrew *nephesh*, meaning animal soul, or in Modern English, our subconscious. Here, however, I am referring the individualization of El as in IS-RA-EL in which EL symbolizes the immortal aspect of our being. There is but one Soul, but Its power to individualize Itself is unlimited. For further discussion of the biblical idiom please refer to my essay *Body and Soul*, BEYOND RELIGION I, (Inhousepress 1998, '01, '02). It may be of some interest that Bhagavad-Gita ascribes the same characteristic to Krishna.

shed all our 'lower' bodies. That we must enter the high state of consciousness only after death. Jesus denies that. He not only claims that Heaven is here and now, that it is both within and without, but that we can enter this exalted state of being while in full possession of our five 'bodies'. As mentioned in *logion 16*, the five bodies, or states of consciousness, are the physical, emotional (or imaginative), the causal, the mental and—of course—the spiritual. We, according to Jesus, are not to shed those bodies, but we must *spiritualize* them.

This gives us a most fascinating assurance. Not only we can enjoy Paradise here and now, but after the physical 'death' i.e.: after freeing ourselves of the constraints of our physical body, the nature of Paradise is such that we retain our individuality. Jesus assures us that when entering Paradise we retain the capability, indeed the total command, of all our 'bodies'. We do not dissolve into some sort of spiritual miasma. The five trees are *unmoved in summer or in winter*, they, those five spiritualized states of consciousness can and do exist beyond time and space. Should we so desire, we can thus (ultimately) manifest our presence in any state of consciousness we choose—even the physical.

After all, isn't this what Jesus did?

***

20

The disciples said to Jesus: Tell us what the Kingdom of Heaven is like. He said to them: It is like a mustard-seed, smaller than all seeds. But when it falls on the tilled earth, it produces a large branch and becomes shelter for <the> birds of heaven.

This *logion* hardly needs any comment. The Kingdom of Heaven is an Idea. A tiny idea like a mustard seed. Yet when this tiny idea takes hold of a receptive mind, it grows rejecting all limitations, becomes a powerful state of consciousness in which diverse thoughts (birds of heaven) find shelter.

We are gods.

We have the power to convert virtual potential into tangible reality. We create our own universes. These universes, in turn, generate new ideas, and they grow and expand. There is no end to Infinity.

***

21

Mary said to Jesus: Whom are thy disciples like? He said: They are like little children who have installed themselves in a field which is not theirs. When the owners of the field come, they will say: "Release to us our field". They take off their clothes before them to release it (the field) to them and to give back their field to them. Therefore I say: If the lord of the house knows that the thief is coming he will stay awake before he comes and will not let him dig through into this house of his kingdom to carry his goods. You then must watch for the world, gird up your loins with great strength lest the brigands find (a) way to come to you, because they will find the advantage which you expect. Let there be among you a man of understanding; when the fruit ripened, he came quickly with his sickle in his hand, he reaped it. Whoever has ears to hear let him hear.

Whoever has ears to hear let him hear.

We think that we own what we have. Think again. No amount of legal documentation will allow us to take with us what is not truly ours. And only that is truly ours that we possess fully within our consciousness. And only that consciousness is immortal which is born of Spirit.

And that's that.

When we shed our physical body, we shed our physical consciousness. For the *Owner of the field*, the true Owner of our state of consciousness, our Higher Self, claims what is His. We must take off our clothes before Him. We must shed all our bodies, all our lower states of consciousness, not just the physical but the emotional, causal and mental sheaths. We shed our material goods, all our emotional attachments—our likes and dislikes, all our philosophical hypotheses, suppositions, convictions. We have nothing left. Nothing.

Unless we learn to identify with the true Owner.

Next follows a picturesque description of the same 'problem' from a different perspective. Jesus now examines the event of our physical 'death' from his disciples' point of view. The lord of the house is you and I. The house is our state of consciousness. It is our perceived reality, that in which we abide. We suspect an impending 'death'. We are trying to stay awake. Not to lose consciousness, not to 'die'. We do not want to lose all we have. All that we have accumulated over the years. We must exert great strength not to give in. We must live on... must try again... defend our own.

Let there be a man of understanding among you. [35]

There are five men, five states of consciousness. Let there be one who understands. He who does, let him grow allegiance with the immortal, with the imperishable. Let him guard the fruit of his labors, gather whatever is ripe, ready for harvest and place it where it cannot be lost. Be it emotional imagery, be it through a mental perception, be it by locking it firmly in our subconscious, but it must be raised to the highest, the spiritual level. That which is truly ours, which is anchored in our spiritual consciousness cannot be lost. It is ours forever.

Whoever has ears to hear let him hear.

***

---

[35]   One of the keys to understanding the gospel of Thomas, or any other gospel, is the acceptance that regardless what congregation Jesus addressed at any particular time, his message is always one-on-one. See also my comments to *logion 23*.

22

Jesus saw children who are being suckled. He said to his disciples: These children who are being suckled are like those who enter the Kingdom. They said to Him: Shall we then, being children, enter the Kingdom? Jesus said to them: When you make the inner as the outer and the outer as the inner and the above as the below, and when you make the male and the female into a single one, so that the male will not be male and the female (not) be female, when you make eyes in the place of an eye, and a hand in the place of a hand, and a foot in the place of a foot, (and) an image in the place of an image, then shall you enter [the Kingdom].

The children being suckled are not yet aware of their ego. Ego is that which keeps us from being part of the Whole.

When you make the inner as the outer, etc. This is another lecture on the nature of God, or at least on the nature of divinity. We live in a world that by definition is a world of duality. The inner and the outer, the above and the below, the male and the female, are all facet of a dualistic world. The purpose of dualism, or the consciousness of contrasts, is to accelerate our learning process. It is much easier to assess the value of something in relation to something else than to perceive an intrinsic value without anything to compare it to. Someone once defined God as That which the opposites have in common. A simple sentence, a difficult concept. And yet God is the Infinite Source of *everything*. Those who assign reality to the 'devil' are not true believers in monotheism. Emmet Fox, the late teacher and healer, said that evil has no reality unless we choose to give it such. One could say that it is an absence rather than a presence. According to Jesus there is only One Reality. God. There is none other. And therefore we must unify the opposites within our consciousness. We must eliminate any thought or feeling of dualism. We must even get rid of opinions for or against.

Judge not, that ye be not judged.[36] (N.B.: We should not confuse judgment with discrimination which must be practiced vigilantly at all times). Judgment, an expression of an opinion, is an exercise in dualism. Whereas there is only the One, Eternal, Infinite, Almighty Oneness.

That is the first part of this *logion*. The second deals with our spiritual body.

Most of us seem to be willing to accept that there maybe some sort of ethereal, highly diluted spiritualistic soul-type emanation which can percolate through the walls, hover at the brink of our awareness and then return to the invisible worlds. Unfortunately, if this is what we believe, this will be what we'll get. We create our own universes, remember?

What Jesus teaches in this *logion* is something quite different. According to Jesus we must create a spiritual reality as solid, as concrete as that which we experience every day with our physical senses. We must fully, unreservedly, without the least shadow of doubt, accept—ney—*create* a spiritual body with spiritual eyes, hands, feet, all the senses; an inner body, a state of consciousness, in which images are as real as any image in this, physical world.[37]

It is my contention that when Jesus healed, he saw the inner bodies of those seeking his help. He cured that which he saw with His spiritual eyes, he adjusted the inner images. The rest was only a consequence.

When those inner images become real, we enter the Kingdom.

***

---

[36]   Matthew 7:1 [Note: the main object lesson in this quotation is the consequence of acquiring karma, but the aspect of dualistic thought remains].
[37]   The inner spiritual body already exists, of course, however it is not part of the reality in which we choose to have our being.

23

Jesus said: I shall choose you, one out of a thousand, and two out of ten thousand, and they shall stand as a single one.*
   *"single one" same as "solitary" in *logion 16*

I shall choose *you*. Whom is Jesus addressing? What is the reality in which Jesus has His being? As said before, we are a state of consciousness. Each time we change our viewpoint, each time a new thought crosses our mind, it changes our awareness. We enter a different state. A different reality.

We are a mess.

Most of the time we have little or no control over our thoughts, let alone over what subconscious reaction we have to them. A thousand states, perhaps ten thousand might pass as fleetingly as a blink of an eye; one or two may be of value, but ultimately they must stand as a single one. A single state of consciousness from which all others emanate.

To understand Jesus' teaching we might do well to remember that He never addressed thousands of people, even if thousands had been present. He always tried to contact each, individual soul. One on one.

***

24

His disciples said: Show us the place where Thou art, for it is necessary for us to seek it. He said to them: Whoever has ears let him hear. Within a man of light there is light and he lights the whole world. When he does not shine, there is darkness.

Poor disciples. They still have no idea. No wonder Jesus almost ignores the question. He already answered it so many times. Yet His patience is truly divine. He finds yet another way of saying the same truth.

Within spiritual consciousness knowledge abounds. It fills up all its aspects, all its world, all its being. If this spiritual awareness withdraws from our perception, there is ignorance. We must at all times abide in the highest consciousness of which we are capable. Not just on Sundays, or later... when we are not, ah... so busy? Or, perhaps, when we get to be a little older?

Otherwise there is darkness. Ignorance.

Death.

***

25

Jesus said: Love thy brother as thy soul, guard him as the apple of thine eye.
　　　(Transl. comment) **"apple"**; lit.: **"pupil"**.

　　　Why? Why is it so necessary to be so concerned about other people? *Am I my brother's keeper?* asks disgruntled Cain.[38]   According to Jesus—we are.
　　　Why?
　　　There are two ways of looking at evolution. Both of them spiritual. The first is to grow oneself; to reach unity with one's own Higher Self. To reach the level at which we can say: *I and my Father are one.*[39] To become a co-worker with the divine within us. This might be described as Self-Realization.

　　　But there is a further, even deeper understanding of the Oneness of the Divine. In the ultimate sense, we are all One. Why? Because we are all divergent expressions of the one God. Paul in his letter to Ephesians elucidates this concept even further; he points out: *One God and Father of all, who is above all, and through all, and in you all.*[40] In this sense, none of us can reach spiritual maturity until all of us do so. Ego is that which sets us apart. The Spirit is that which brings us together. It is true that we are all individual souls. But individual means not only unique but also indivisible,

---

[38]　　Genesis 4:9
[39]　　John 10:30. Note the order of the words. "I and my Father", not "My Father and I". This order is upheld in The New King James Version. [God has no being other than in a mode of being].
[40]　　Ephesians 4:6

inseparable, from Latin *individuus*. From this point of view your brother is as much part of you as is the pupil in your own eye. Your spiritual eye. Your spiritual state of consciousness.

We are all—ONE.

***

26

Jesus said: The mote that is in thy brother's eye thou seest, but the beam that is in thine eye, thou seest not. When thou castest the beam out of thine eye, then thou wilt see clearly to cast the mote out of thy brother's eye.

Surely this is one of those rare sentences that no one can misunderstand.

To put it in a different context, let us imagine a teenager brought up in the back-streets of Calcutta. Or the favelas of Saõ Paulo. Or the darkest recesses of New York city. Can we really judge those youngsters by the same yardstick as we would someone who inherited creature comforts from his or her parents? Surely for the poorest of the poor it is a superb effort of will, of self-denial, of consideration for another *not* to steal. Not to steal to sustain one's body and soul—together. To survive.

There is one other thing. We are all born into conditions (states of consciousness) ideal for our own personal, individual growth. What may seem strange to one, may be vital to another. We simply do not know. We are simply in no position of judge. The sentiment of this *logion* is stated even more clearly in other Scriptures quoted before: Judge *not, that ye be not judged.*[41] There is an ancient occult law that states that "like attracts like". If we judge, we shall be judged. If we forgive, we shall be forgiven. If we love, we shall be loved. And so on. It's our choice.

***

---

[41]   Luke 6:37

27

<Jesus said:> If you fast not from the world, you will not find the Kingdom; if you keep not the Sabbath as Sabbath,* you will not see the Father.
*(Transl. comment) **"keep... as Sabbath"** lit.: **"make into Sabbath"**

This business of fasting keeps coming back, although when Jesus uses the word, He refers, as always, to the spiritual meaning. To fast from the world is to refrain from paying undue attention to the physical universe and all its trappings. It is not to allow ourselves to become attached to things material, things transient and therefore unreal.

The Sabbath is a different matter altogether. The day of rest is not a day during which we are to waste our time by watching TV or going to a football match (after meeting our friend just outside the church, of course!). We can make into a Sabbath any day, any hour, any minute of our life. It is the moment-in-time, a fragment of eternity, when we stop being preoccupied with action, with things requiring activity of body or mind, with movement, and seek out that great immovable silence within our heart wherein we just listen. Or watch. It is the moment when we invite the True Reality to take over. Very gently. It is that moment in our life when time no longer matters, when all laws of the physical universe are suspended, are held in abeyance. It is when we ask for nothing, even thank for nothing, though we seem imbued with a grateful heart. It is a moment when we just are. When we enter the True Reality.

***

28

Jesus said: I took my stand in the midst of the world and in flesh I appeared to them; I found them all drunk, I found none among them athirst. And my soul was afflicted for the sons of men, because they are blind in their heart and do not see that* empty they have come into the world (and that) empty they seek to go out of the world again. But now they are drunk. When they have shaken off their wine, then will they repent.

   *(Transl. comment) **"that"** or **"because"**

A plaintive cry from a Man who had so much to give and none were there to receive.

Here again Jesus speaks from the level of His spiritual consciousness, as His own Higher Self. This state of awareness became known as the Christ Consciousness.

"I have assumed human, physical form for their sakes, yet none of them thirst for my knowledge," He seems to be saying. [42] "But what really hurts my soul is that they are not even aware of their own ignorance. People who are drunk are not capable of discerning the vicissitudes of material, let alone spiritual reality. They were born with a clean slate, with all the opportunities, and yet, they've done nothing with their lives. [43] Empty will they die. They

---

[42]   Meaning, "I have reincarnated myself". It should be recognized that it is always the Higher Self who chooses Its (His) own embodiment. We are not born into any given conditions by accident, but by an incredibly detailed program, designed to expedite our spiritual growth. Whether we take advantage of it or not, is our decision.

[43]   There is a reason for being born without remembering one's past lives. Few people can cope with their present problems. "Sufficient unto

are drank with their own self-importance, their own ignorance. Until they give up their false beliefs, their attachments, they will not accept My way."

If Jesus were to address us today, how would he change such a statement? Would he simply change the pronoun *they* to *you*? And *their* for *yours*?

How many of us, I wonder, are prepared to give up our pet theories, our ego boosting mental garbage and accept the reality of spiritual life? How many of those who call themselves Christians, I wonder, are prepared to do it?

***

the day is the evil thereof," says Jesus in Matthew 6:34. Let alone the evil of one life.

29

Jesus said: If the flesh has come into existence because of *the* spirit, it is a marvel; but if <the> spirit (has come into existence) because of the body, it is a marvel of marvels. But I marvel at how this great wealth has made its home in this poverty.

The philosopher's conundrum: is the mind the byproduct of the brain, or the brain the byproduct of the mind. Likewise with the Spirit. Did the Spirit beget the material universe, or did the world happen by an inexplicable accident, and then evolved, due to unforeseen circumstances, into an awareness of Spirit? This question touches on the principles underlying the creative process itself. Does the Idea precede it's fulfillment, or is everything a meaningless charade of disjointed, senseless aberrations of fate.

I prefer the first option. To those who identify Jesus with some preconceived, stringent religious or philosophical tenets should reread this *logion* carefully. Jesus does not even state that any external or divine force must be responsible for the creation of the universe. "Could the body have evolved a Spirit?" He wanders. Whatever happened to the old, dualistic god of the Old Testament? Or at least of the fundamentalist's interpretation of the O.T.. Jesus had obviously outgrown the Hebrew concept of God. But whatever the conclusion, one cannot but share the wonderment that Jesus felt by observing the marvel of creation being manifested in and through such humble 'poverty' as the human flesh and blood.

***

30

Jesus said: Where there are three gods, they are gods; where there are two or one, I am with him.

This is truly a mysterious statement. The three gods refer to the mystical symbolism inherent of the word *Israel*. The three gods are the three powers expressed by the *Is*: the feminine principle, *Ra*: the masculine principle, and *El*: the divine principle or the wholeness of trinity.[44] Thus if the three coexist together, the three gods under the unifying force of the *El*, the completeness has been achieved, i.e.: the three became One.

If only two or even one have heretofore developed a semblance of spiritual awareness, Jesus (speaking as the Higher Self) steps in as the unifying principle. He is the El, the Divine Spark, which spiritualizes and unifies the two lower principles.

One should note the gender of pronoun in *"I am with him."* It appears expedient that Jesus as the *El* is with *him*, with the conscious, positive or the masculine principle. This factor may lie at the root of the reticence of most of the so-called Christian churches to afford their women adherent equal rights. In fact this principle is totally misunderstood. As we shall see in later *logia*, both the male

---

[44]   For those to whom it may be of interest: *Is* is the corruption of the Egyptian goddess Isis who, in addition to representing the feminine principle, also symbolizes the passive or the subconscious. In the Hebrew tradition the word *nephesh* translated as soul, strictly means the *animal soul*, as against the *El* that would represent the immortal Soul. *Ra*, the Egyptian sun god, in addition to symbolizing the masculine principle, also represents the positive, conscious mind.

and the female principles must be made subservient to the Higher Self which, of course, is neither male nor female.

***

31

Jesus said: No prophet is acceptable in his village, no physician heals those who know him.

We invariably expect the grass to be greener over the next hill. We also seem to expect the messengers of God to be very 'extraordinary' people; perhaps taller than average, beautifully built with wise, calm, features, a regal bearing, and definitely with an aura of sanctity oozing all around them. We seem to forget that it is not we who choose to represent the Divine, but it is the Divine that chooses Its messengers. Albeit we must cooperate if the Higher Self is to fulfill Its mission. Whatever it might be.

I am reminded of Salieri's reaction to the youthful Mozart in the 1984 film *Amadeus*. According to the film, Salieri, the established, important, if rather pompous, principal composer to the Imperial Court recognizes Mozart's genius, but he cannot understand why God would grant such divine talent to an obnoxious, juvenile, undisciplined pip-squeak. He forgets that it had not been Mozart's purpose to act as an *arbiter elegantiarum* to the Imperial Court, but to act as a transmuter for the celestial music and to 'spread' its message to the world. By the time of his death, the youthful thirty-five years old Mozart had proven more prolific than all his contemporaries twice his age.

One can but wonder if we would accept Mozart's compositions had he been born in our era—of electronically amplified noise that passes nowadays for music. Perhaps no more so than the wisdom of the gospel of Thomas?

***

32

Jesus said: A city being built on a high mountain (and) fortified can not fall nor can it (ever) be hidden.

A city symbolizes a state of consciousness. The high mountain symbolizes the raising of such a consciousness to a high level. The countless martyrs throughout history attest to the thesis that such a 'city' cannot fall.[45] Also, such a high state of consciousness can never be hidden. People seem drawn to it (often having no idea why) be it to learn, be it to oppose it, but rarely to ignore it.

***

---

[45]   The original meaning of the word martyr was (also) witness.

33

Jesus said: What thou shalt hear in thine ear (and) in the other ear, that preach from your housetops: for no one lights a lamp and puts it under a bushel, nor does he put it in a hidden place, but he sets it on the lampstand, so that all who come in and go out may see the light.

...and in the other ear: "the spiritual ear that shares with all willing to listen. For he that divulges such knowledge does not do so to edify a single one, but to share it with all who are ready to receive it. For there is no hidden knowledge. So that all who go into their inner sanctum and come out again might have access to this knowledge."

We must never forget that light, in the biblical idiom, invariably symbolizes knowledge.

It is very important to understand that Jesus appears to insist that, contrary to some mystery religions' contention, he that receives higher knowledge is obliged to share it with others. This must be reconciled with a statement elsewhere in the Scriptures that one should not *cast pearls before swine*.[46] I would suggest, however, that it is our ability to absorb knowledge that defines it as esoteric, not the nature of knowledge itself. Or, as Thomas Aquinas put it: *Whatever is received is received according to the nature of the recipient.*

That is to say that whoever is not ready to receive such pearls of knowledge will reject it until such a time as he or she matures into a receptive attitude. Thus such jewels of wisdom (higher

---

46   Matthew 7:6

knowledge) should be always offered but never imposed, *lest they* (who are not as yet ready to receive them) *trample them under their feet.*[47]

Nevertheless, as Einstein would say, all things are relative. In the Apocryphal Acts John had this to say about a lamp:

> *A lamp am I to you that perceive me*
> *A mirror am I to you that know me*

***

---

[47]   ibid. It is interesting to note that there is little evidence in the New Testament or Gnostic writings, that Jesus involved Himself in arguments, polemics or philosophical dialectics. He announced the 'good news' and went on, seeking receptive minds.

34

Jesus said: If a blind man leads a blind man, both of them fall into a pit.

The state of the world today, the 'average' level of consciousness illustrates this *logion* better than any comment I might make. We choose our leaders. We deserve them.

***

35

Jesus said: It is not possible for one to enter the house of the strong Man and take him (or: it) by force unless he bind his hand; then will he ransack his house.

The house (as any place in which one abides, e.g.: the city, town, village, tent etc.) symbolizes a state of consciousness. The *hand* symbolizes the power to effect manifestation (to be creative, to have executive power) and/or the ability to express spiritual ideas at the physical plane of awareness.[48] More precisely, in this case, the *hand* symbolizes the male, or the positive awareness.[49]

The *logion* states that unless one distracts or otherwise incapacitates one's sound judgment (by psychological trickery, so well known to all the secret police forces of the world, or by hypnosis, brainwashing, drugs incl. alcohol, or by poisoning the young minds, the minds of children before they had a chance to learn discrimination), we cannot adversely affect one's state of consciousness. The obvious lesson is to avoid any and all circumstances that reduce our control over our mental faculties.

***

---

[48]   DICTIONARY OF BIBLICAL SYMBOLISM, S. Kapuscinski

[49]   see *logion* 30

36

Jesus said: Take no thought from morning until evening and from evening until morning for what you shall put on.

We put on airs, moods, pretenses. We put on a host of personalities for every occasion. Jesus tells us to just be. The Spirit, our Higher Self, will take care of all we need. All we need to learn is to respond to the dictates of that little voice within us. To do so we must become like little children and trust our Father. In all things.

On occasion we may tend to forget that Spirit is beyond time, beyond space, beyond the concepts of our physical universe. Jesus advocates that we live in Spirit. That we live in and for the moment. In and for the instant of the eternal now.

***

37

His disciples said: when wilt Thou be revealed to us and when will we see Thee? Jesus said: When you take off your clothing without being ashamed, and take your clothes and put them under your feet as the little children and tread on them, then [shall you behold] the Son of the Living (One) and you shall not fear.

*(Translator's comment) or: **"when you take off your shame"**

Jesus teaches the same Truth in a thousand different ways. To attempt to translate His teaching into today's language, one must unavoidably repeat oneself. Thus, here Jesus reiterates, yet again, that when we remove our mortal personality, our mental and emotional baggage, our airs and pretenses, all of which constitute our ego—then, and only then, can we aspire to see with our spiritual eyes that which is spiritual. Until such a time, we are looking at the Truth through frosted glass of our conditioning, of our accumulated dross that pervades and pollutes our subconscious. The apostle Paul describes our present and future abilities as follows: for *now we see through a glass, darkly (or, in a riddle); but then shall I know even as also I am known.*[50]

It is evident that once we become aware of our true Self, we shall no longer be afraid of the Son of the Living One. Most fears originate, often by a complex psychological route, in our fear of death. When we recognize the "Son of the living One," we recognize our own immortality. All our fears dissipate forever.

Some of us might experience considerable anxiety when

---

[50]   1 Corinthians 13:12

coming face to face with the true nature of our being. We might
think that to equate oneself with an immortal entity within us is
paramount to blasphemy. Nevertheless Jesus advocated, pleaded
and commanded us to take just such a course of self-discovery.
Perhaps it should be mentioned that contrary to the teachings of
Christian religions, the Father in Heaven is *not* God. He is the
'emanation' of God.[51] He symbolizes the Living Spirit that emanates from God and manifests as *El*, the immortal Soul.[52] By becoming one with the Spirit within us we become as gods. Not as
God.

***

---

[51]   While I would never encourage anyone to enter the murky corri-
dors of esoteric theology, for the aficionados of such a course I offer my
essay on *Trinity* in my collection of essays: BEYOND RELIGION III
(Inhousepress 2001, '02)

[52]   See commentary to *Logion* 30. Perhaps I should stress again the
importance of not confusing 'soul' translated from Hebrew *nephesh*,
meaning *animal soul*, i.e.: the subconscious mind, and 'Soul', the *Higher
Self*, the immortal *El*. Perhaps a degree of confusion is unavoidable since
we are directed to sanctify our soul until it becomes one with that within
us which is immortal. Thus ultimately soul and Soul become one.

38

Jesus said: Many times have you desired to hear these words which I say to you, and you have no other from whom to hear them. There will be days when you will seek Me (and) you will not find Me.

We have all experienced that nagging hunger, on occasion. We have days, moments, when we are tired of our lot, of the world we live in. We seem to think that there must be a better way to run this universe, this country, the business we are in, the family we created... a better way to live. We search our minds, our hearts, our souls—all to no avail. We seem stuck in a rut. We are held there by an apparently indomitable force of nature. Verdi called it *La Forza del destino*. The force of destiny. We feel there is no one who can help us. Mystics call this state the dark side (or the night) of the soul.

This state of abandonment is, of course, an illusion. A self-imposed, transient condition. Yet we feel that we are all alone.

We don't have to be.

***

39

Jesus said: The Pharisees and Scribes have received the keys of Knowledge, they have hidden them. They did not enter, and they did not let those (enter) who wished. But you, become wise as serpents and innocent as doves.

The Pharisees and Scribes had been the recognized religious leaders. According to Jesus, they knew how to raise their own state of consciousness. They also knew how to help others to do so. They did neither. Perhaps they knew that the moment the ordinary people discover the secret of the Kingdom within, they would become independent; that they, the religious leaders, would no longer be able to control them.

Jesus tells his followers to learn discrimination on their own, to turn in all innocence to the deep silence within and there to seek the Truth. According to Jesus, in His day, the ordinary folk could not count on their priesthood for guidance.

Can we?

***

40

Jesus said: A vine has been planted without the Father and, as it is not established, it will be pulled up by its roots and be destroyed.

Any state of consciousness that we develop without taking our spiritual nature into account will not last. It would be like building a house without foundations.

***

41

Jesus said: Whoever has in his hand, to him shall be given; and whoever does not have, from him shall be taken even the little which he has.

Whoever has in his hand... what?

Whoever has the keys. The keys to the Kingdom.

We seem to need constant remainders that Jesus taught *only* spiritual truth. *Render to Caesar the things that are Caesar's.*[53] Jesus does not deny, condemn or forbid our dealings in or with the physical world. He simply states, repeatedly, that He has no interest in it. That if we want to accumulate material riches then it's our business. He only warns us that such riches are transient. We can't keep them. We can't take them with us. They will not give us more than temporary, shallow, illusion of happiness. But... "it's your business," He seems to be saying. "Don't bother Me with it."

If, however, we seek the indestructible reality, if we seek that which is completely independent of the wiles of the physical world, then we shall listen when He says: Come *unto me, all ye that labor and are heavy laden, and I will give you rest.*[54] It is almost as if He was saying: "I'll teach you a trick how to become free. How to find an incredible source of happiness that can never let you down... And what's more, here's another thing: If you just start on the right way, your true, indestructible riches will grow, they will multiply."

"There is no end to this," He seems to assure us. "My source is infinite. On the other hand, if you don't, if you only judge suc-

---

[53]   Mark 12:17 et al.

[54]   Matthew 11:28

cess in physical, material terms, then, even what little you have you will lose. It is only a question of time. All material things are transient."

This is what He is saying to me.

What do you think?

***

42

Jesus said: Become passers-by.

An immortal soul (our true Self) assumes a human form. Usually it spends a few years learning the skills of physical survival and then reverts to those aspects that are imperative for its advancement on the ladder of spiritual evolution. When the specific lesson assigned for the particular embodiment is learned, the soul sheds the body, which it had created for this specific purpose, and returns to its more permanent abode.

Not to the 'ultimate' heaven. There is no such thing.[55]

Heaven is a state of consciousness and, as Jesus had never tired of repeating, it is within us. Not within our *physical* body, but within our state of consciousness, which, if imbued with spiritual qualities, becomes integrated with our immortal Self, which constitutes our spiritual body.

Furthermore, there is no limit to the expansion of our consciousness. If the soul developed new interests in matters which it "*can* take with it", then the duration between physical reincarnations lasts longer. According to some mystics, it can last up to the equivalent of a thousand or two of our earthly years. There, in that non-physical reality, our Self, or soul, continues to develop its heightened perception of Truth. It works on the seeds that had been planted on fertile soil, here, on earth.

If a soul on its stopover within material reality has been only

---

[55]   The danger always lies in the premise that whatever we believe in defines our reality. The admonition in *logion 44* is particularly adamant on this subject. Misconceptions can cause prolonged periods of relative stasis in our development.

vaguely interested (if at all) in the matters of spirit, than its sojourn in *Bardo* is likely to be very short.[56] It would have little to dwell on. It would return quickly to assume another body and, hopefully, try harder.

Nevertheless, we are not urged to make our stay on earth either long or short, regardless of the duration of our sojourn in *Bardo*.[57] But we are urged to recognize our sojourn on earth, or within material reality, for what it is. A transient state of becoming. We are also told not to get obsessively involved with "things that are Caesar's." Once we step on the spiritual path, they do not really concern us. We enjoy them, appreciate them, even rejoice in them, but... we do not lose sleep over them.

We are in—but not *of* this world.

Here, on earth, we are passers-by.

***

---

[56]   'Bardo' is one of many names given to the more permanent (though still transient) residence of our inner self. Bercholz and Kohn in ENTERING THE STREAM (An Overview of Schools of Buddhism) define it as of Tibetan origins: "Intermediate state between death and the next rebirth or another of the transitional states of experience"

[57]   There appears to be a reason for this apparent omission. It seems that people who are intent on their spiritual development may, under special circumstances, fulfill the equivalent of two or more 'incarnations' in a single physical lifetime. What really takes place is a fundamental change in their consciousness. The rules, however, do not change. Each 'phase' must be carried to its fulfillment and in each phase one remains no more than a passer-by.

43

His disciples said to Him: Who art Thou that Thou should say these things to us. <Jesus said to them:> From what I say to you, you do not know who I am, but you have become as the Jews, for they love the tree, they hate its fruit and they love the fruit, they hate the tree.

They love the idea of being gods, but they hate what it entails. They hate the responsibilities, the commitment, the presumed sacrifices, and particularly the necessary detachment from all things material. Or... they love the benefits, the gifts of the Spirit (the freedom, the peace of mind, the knowledge, the power to heal, to prophesy etc.), but they hate Him who possesses such powers. Jealousy? Ego raising its ugly head? And yet the gifts of the Spirit are the corollary, the natural unavoidable fruit of the commitment to the spiritual life. They are the other side of the same coin.

I doubt if only the Jews[58] have this problem.

***

---

[58] Jews (Yehûdîm) in Hebrew carries two distinct meanings: 1. A descendant of Judah, or 2. "Let Him (God) be praised," implying: "he who praises God." Jesus may well have had the latter meaning in mind, i.e.: "You have become as those who praise God but do not follow His teachings."

44

Jesus said: Whoever blasphemes against the Father, it shall be forgiven him, and whoever blasphemes against the Son, it shall be forgiven him; but whoever blasphemes against the Holy Ghost, it shall not be forgiven him, either on earth or in heaven.

Here we are taken beyond *logion 15*. In *logion 50* Jesus states that we are the children of Light, children born of Spiritual Knowledge. When we become aware of our spiritual nature, of our divine heritage, we become aware of who is our Father. Until then we are groping. By denying our true origin we neither do nor can negate Its existence. Whether we accept of the 'Father,' our Higher Self, or not—It (He) is there.

The Son is he has achieved a level of consciousness in which he can no longer differentiate between His Higher Self and his earthly personality. It is an individual, a spiritual entity, whose relationship to the world, as we know it, has become *impersonal.* Such an entity has become indestructible, by our standards— immutable, whether or not we give credence to It. [59] It is the coming of age. Spiritual maturity is reached when the Infinite finds expression through the particular. Thus Jesus' individuality could not die at the termination of His stay here, on earth. Nor is His immortality affected by our beliefs.

The Holy Ghost, or Spirit, is a different concept altogether. Spirit is that of which all things are made. It is Life Itself. By denying the Spirit, by blaspheming against It, we are denying the Real-

---

[59]   Immutable by 'our standards'—but the spiritual evolution, of course, goes on; beyond the earth, beyond the limitations we can conceive of. After all, God is infinite and we are gods, i.e. created in Its (His) image.

ity Itself. By not recognizing the true reality we are as though we were dead. *Let the dead bury the dead,* says Jesus, to a man who wanted to bury his father's mortal remains before stepping onto the spiritual path.[60] He, that man, still recognized the physical reality as *the* reality. By delaying an immediate response to Jesus' call, the man denied his own very existence. He hadn't been born yet. According to Jesus, any man who discerns True Reality, the reality of Spirit, and looks back, ...*is not fit for the kingdom of God.*[61]

***

---

[60]   Luke 9:60

[61]   Luke 9:62

45

Jesus said: They do not harvest grapes from thorns, nor do they gather figs from thistles; [for] they give no fruit. [A] good man brings forth good out of his treasure, an evil man brings forth evil things out of his evil treasure, which is in his heart, and speaks evil things. For out of the abundance of the heart he brings forth evil things.

The substance of this *logion* is self-evident. The abundance of man's heart is the consciousness he has developed, with particular reference to his subconscious mind.[62]

Below, a few thoughts on the consequences of this philosophy:

It is evident that we must concentrate on the process, though we are judged by results. The process is the search for the Kingdom; the results are the 'good' deeds.

Anyone who says, "do as I say," instead of "do as I do," is not a follower of Jesus' teaching. Any man who preaches forgiveness but hardens his heart against him who did him injustice is not a follower of Jesus.

And so on.

Why? Why should we not punish those who have hurt us? The apostle Paul repeats the wonderfully poetic words recurring throughout the Old Testament: Vengeance *is mine; I will repay, saith the Lord.*[63] So who is this Lord who punishes the guilty? Surely not the all-loving, all forgiving Deity who is Love Itself?

Surely not. To understand the concept of justice we must ex-

---

[62]   i.e. *nephesh*, usually translated as soul.
[63]   Romans 12:19

amine the concept of the so called: *karma*. A 'good' man will generate 'good' karma, an 'evil' man 'bad' karma. Each according to his (acquired) nature. 'Good' is always directed towards spiritualization of our consciousness, 'bad' results in material illusions. 'Good' is almost any action, since we learn from our mistakes, 'bad' is stagnation, laziness, indifference. "*I would thou wert cold or hot.*"[64]

A great deal has been written on the subject. A great deal more shall be written. For the purposes of understanding the concept, however, we can defer to pure physics: every action has an equal and opposite reaction. If we accept this concept in the physical or material world, then what of the worlds within? A complementary esoteric law states: As above, so below, or *...whatsoever thou shalt bind on earth shall be bound in heaven: and whatsoever thou shalt loose on earth shall be loosed in heaven.*[65] That's the key but also the consequence.

This tenet makes the law of karmic retribution infinitely exacting. We have already learned that Heaven is a state of consciousness. Such a state is expressed in our physical, emotional and mental attitudes. As such not only any and all physical harms we may have perpetrated on our neighbor must be rectified, but also any mental or emotional injustices we have committed shall hunt us until the state of balance is restored. If we hate (anyone for any reason) we shall be hated. An equal and opposite reaction. If we consider our way better than another's, our own way shall be looked down upon. God, it has been said, is what the opposites have in common. It is a state of balance, equilibrium. We must restore this state within our own consciousness in order to restore our place within the Kingdom.

There seems only one way to protect oneself from the repercussions of this immutable law. Jesus put it this way: *...whatsoever ye would that men should do to you, do ye even so to them: for this*

---

[64]   Revelation 3:15. The next verse continues: "*...because thou art lukewarm, and neither cold nor hot, I will spue thee out of my mouth.*"
[65]   Matthew 16:19

is the law and the prophets.[66] The golden rule. We shall *always* taste our own medicine. The law seems inbreed into our genes.

And thus, we have no need to extract vengeance. It will be done for us. The law is equally prevalent in all realities. Material, emotional and mental. (In spiritual reality the state of balance has already been reached). Sometimes it may take a while. The law is impersonal and infinitely patient. Its long arms stretch to infinity.

Alas... we are immortal.

It will happen.

***

---

[66]   Matthew 7:12

46

Jesus said: From Adam until John the Baptist there is among those who are born of women none higher than John the Baptist, so that his eyes will not be broken. But I have said that whoever among you becomes as a child shall know the Kingdom, and he shall become higher than John.

At face value, a strange statement to say the least. John the Baptist, who has given up all his worldly domains to prepare for the coming of the Lord, is less than anyone who becomes as a child? Taking the *logia* (or any part of the Bible) literally can be very frustrating!

We must again return to first principles.

The physical, emotional and mental 'bodies' are all constituents of the material worlds. Only Higher Self, the Spirit, is exempt from this classification. Jesus is saying that John the Baptist went as far as anyone can by using his physical, emotional and mental faculties. What he, John, had *not* done was to stop suffering, to stop preaching (telling others what to do), to stop living in the desert and denying himself the gifts of the spirit. Or simply... to start enjoying life.[67] Like a little child. A child who has perfect faith that its mother and father, or indeed someone can, and will, sate all its needs.

All people I've met, particularly those who expressed some interest in religions or, better still, in spiritual life, invariably appeared to think that Jesus "came to earth" to create a religion, most explicitly based on self-sacrifice and self-denial. Nothing could be further from the truth. Jesus not only fought His contemporary re-

---

[67] Perhaps it should be repeated that Jesus had never suggested that we should stop enjoying life. Just the contrary. He had warned us, however, against forming undue attachment to things that are transient.

ligious hierarchy, but also stated openly that he is in direct opposition to it. *Behold, I make all things new,* John asserts, vigorously, in his Revelation.[68] All things. Apparently we must forget everything we know. It seems that we managed to misunderstand everything that had been promulgated by the prophets. At any rate, this is what Jesus said to His contemporaries. I wonder what He would say to us, today.

As for self-sacrifice and denial, let us remember His words: "These things have I spoken unto you, that *my joy might remain in you,* and *that your joy might be full.*" Or, "I bring you good *tidings of great joy.*"[69] Not much sacrifice or denial in these words.

There are many other examples.

Jesus never intended to create a new religion. He taught us how to *live*, now, today, not how to die. He declared what *is* not what might be—one day—after our physical demise. He just wanted to open our eyes to a new perception of reality. A malleable reality that responds to the dictates of spirit.

***

---

[68]   Revelation 21:5
[69]   John 15:11 and Luke 2:10, et al. (my emphasis)

47

Jesus said: It is impossible for a man to mount two horses and to stretch two bows, and it is impossible for a servant to serve two masters, otherwise he will honour the one and offend the other. No man drinks old wine and immediately desires to drink new wine; and they do not put new (wine into old wineskins), lest they burst, and they do not put old wine into a new wineskins, lest it spoil it. They do not sew an old patch on a new garment, because there would come a rent.

This *logion* seems one of few in which the intent and the meaning are self-evident. There is one phrase, however, which warrants closer scrutiny: No *man drinks old wine and **immediately** desires to drink new wine*. This seems extremely important. We imagine that we can change religions, change our mind-set immediately. At will. So many missionaries appear to think so. Jesus didn't.

In fact, between abandoning any set of tenets, any code of ethics that heretofore guided if not controlled our lives (our state of consciousness), we must, according to Jesus, go through a period best described as apostasy. Rather than jumping from one bandwagon to another, the need presumably precipitated by a feeling of loneliness or alienation, we must step aside, hold our breath, let the old wine (the old knowledge) evaporate. Only when we are free of *emotional* attachments to the old creed, the old mindset, can we absorb new teaching. The period of apostasy will vary from person to person.

Mine lasted almost twenty years.

It is not an easy period, but it does teach us to stand up on our own two (spiritual) feet. It teaches us discrimination, and to assume responsibility for our actions. We learn that there is no one to blame for our condition in life. We learn that each one of us is the sum-total of all that we have ever been. There are no parents,

nor priests, nor rabbis, nor elders, nor other very reverent gentle-
men who can assume the culpability for our mistakes. Not even a
Savior who, with a magic wand, will expunge the consequences of
all our personal blunders. Even without reading any scriptures, we
learn that *God is not mocked: for whatsoever a man soweth, that
shall he also reap.*[70]   The immutable law of karma. We learn that
we are on our own.

It is a process of growing up.

But there again, we are never really alone, are we?

***

---

[70]   Galatians 6:7

48

Jesus said: If two make peace with each other in this house, they shall say to the mountain: "Be moved", and it shall be moved.

This is a *logion* that most people choose to either ignore or to misunderstand. Jesus never intended to defy the laws of gravity nor to indulge in heavy engineering by moving mountains nor, as some other Scriptures imply, to throw them into the sea.[71] It appears that we must be constantly reminded that Jesus taught *spiritual* truth and not its application nor even implication in the physical universe.

The *house* is where we, each one of us, abide, i.e.: our individual state of consciousness. The *two* are the masculine and feminine principles encoded within each one of us, known also as the active and passive aspects, or the animus and anima. If the *two make peace*, they (the dual aspects of our nature) enter into a state of Sabbath: they (we) achieve a higher state of consciousness. The *mountain* always symbolizes such a condition of raised consciousness. See previous *logia*. Moving the mountain simply means having the ability to raise our center of attention. To gain a greater perspective, as when regarding the world from a mountaintop. At such a level of consciousness we can indeed move our awareness, our spiritual body at will.

To recapitulate, the preconditions for changing and elevating our awareness, our state of consciousness, our soul, are:

1. A state of absolute peace, i.e.: a state in which we divorce ourselves from the inputs of our (physical and emotional) senses;

---

[71]   Matthew 21:21, Mark 11:23 et al.

and:

2. The raising of our consciousness, a condition normally associated with a contemplative activity. The two are, in fact, one.

One can only conclude, that we must strive towards existing in this condition all the time, i.e.: of living in a state of full (or raised) consciousness. I simply call it "living consciously". When we perform most daily acts we tend to act as automatons. We do not act, we *react*. Yet even a reaction should be a conscious act. After all, it is the conscious placing of our attention on anything at all that defines our state of being.

To move mountains is to travel in full consciousness. To travel in the spiritual body, in our soul.

***

49

Jesus said: Blessed are the solitary and elect, for you shall find the Kingdom; because you came from it, (and) you shall go there again.

The word *'solitary'* applies to our spiritual nature, it defines our center of interest. The *'elect'* symbolize the state of consciousness in which we have elected to be single-minded. Only those, according to Jesus, will find the Kingdom.

Because you came from it...
Here Jesus talks about the state of consciousness we enjoyed before our original embodiment, a state to which we shall return. Let us never forget that Jesus thinks of us as souls, as Princes aspiring to the Kingdom: not as mortal, transient beings. If we forget this single aspect we shall never understand His teaching.

***

50

**Jesus said: If they say to you: "From where have you origi-
nated?", say to them: "We have come from the Light, where
the Light has originated through itself. It [stood] and it revealed itself in their image". If they say to you: "(Who) are
you?"*, say: "We are His sons and we are the elect of the Living Father". If they ask you: "What is the sign of your Father
in you?", say to them: "It is a movement and a rest".[72]**

*(Transl. comments) "(Who) are you?" ms. "It is you".

This *logion* is a gold mine of information. What is our origin? We have come from the Light. What is light? Light is the
source of all knowledge. Where did it come from? It originated
through itself. This last statement is the enigma, which even Jesus
seemed unwilling to tackle. Perhaps because the consciousness of
the people of His day would have been totally incapable of accept-
ing any explanation.[73]

God is One. Whole. Totality. The single, infinite, inexhaustible Source. Philosophically: a concept without end. However, when

---

[72]   As this *logion* appears to be of a particularly complex structure, the
reader may wish to examine an alternative translation offered by Thomas
O. Lambdin in the Nag Hammadi Library publication: Jesus said, "If they
say to you, 'Where did you come from?' say to them, 'We come from the
light, the place where the light came into being on its own accord and established [itself] and became manifest through their image'. If they say to
you, 'Is it you?' say, 'We are its children, and we are the elect of the living father.' If they ask you, 'What is the sign of your father in you?' say
to them, 'It is movement and repose.'"
[73] Today's theoretical physics accept that subatomic particles constantly
wink in and out of existence, in minute fragments of a second. The origin
of these particles is referred to as Virtual Universe. A sort of Plane of Infinite Potential. Or... Heaven?

we talk of God, of the Source, we can actually only talk about the God which (Who) is *manifested*. In other words we can recognize God in Its creation. I am not limiting this to the physical creation. We can talk of thought, of beauty, of love, of all aspects of God that can be described or put into words. But isn't this the very limitation which we, humans, place on God? Surely we all accept there is more to God than what we can conceive of today. Or, perhaps, ever.

This 'future' concept, future extending to infinity, is the (as yet) *unmanifested* God. It is like a symphony extant in the mind of a composer before he put it on paper, let alone performed it with an orchestra. For that which is *not* manifested we can find no words to describe, no ideas to visualize, no symbols to represent, no concepts to define. It is that which both exists and doesn't, which is and isn't, which always has been yet is still to be, which is what the opposites have in common. It might be thought of as the infinite, indescribable, unimaginable Potential. Baruch Spinoza, a Dutch philosopher of the 17th century said quite simply: To define God is to deny God.[74] He meant that anything we can define is limited by its very definition, whereas God is Infinite.

John (the evangelist) says: He *was in the world, and the world was made by him.*[75] He is saying (at least to me) that the manifested and the unmanifested are two aspects of a single enigma. Enigma because only the manifested God appears to be the Source of knowledge i.e.: Light, yet in order to do so, Light had to have ...*manifested of itself.*

I also contend that this *logion* attests to something new about our own nature. We have already been told that the *El*, the Higher Self that is the Light, the source of all our knowledge, is an immortal indivisible aspect of God. We are now told that this Higher Self has manifested by Itself. Mind boggles at the ramification of this

---

[74]   It may be of interest that for such and similar concepts Spinoza had been excommunicated (in 1656) from the Jewish group in which he was raised. Thus, it may also be of some solace to some that not only Christians suffer from dogmatic constipation. As for Christians, both Catholics and Protestants condemned Spinoza with equal alacrity!

[75]   John 1:10

idea.

We are also told that the Higher Self, Soul, reveals Itself through Its image. That's us. We, the unawakened spiritually, are the image. The reflection. Perhaps not a very good one, as yet, nevertheless we harbor great dormant potential.

The second part of the *logion* deals with the question of who we actually are. The answer is clear: We are the sons of the Living Father. Who is the Living Father? The Manifested Spirit. The Higher Self. The indestructible essence of our consciousness.

Finally, "*What is the sign of the Father in you?*" In us? Let us make very sure that this sign is present within us. If not, Jesus will call us 'the dead'. Spiritually dead. The sign is *a movement and a rest*. We must always remember that it is our own state of consciousness that defines and limits *what* and more particularly *who* we are. We can only be that of which we are aware. Only that which we embrace with our consciousness.

'Movement' is the manifested and 'rest' the unmanifested universe. Life and Potential (Life). The potential of creation. Hence, to quote the Psalmist just once more: "Ye are gods".[76] We are possessed of infinite power to create universes. Within our consciousness. Our Kingdom.

There is yet another way to understand this "movement and the rest." The two define the condition of becoming and of being. Our being is at rest. Our becoming—the movement. We must accept, I feel, that God has no being other than in a mode of being. Apparently we are both. Being and becoming.

***

---

[76]   Psalm 82:6

51

His disciples said to Him: When will the repose of the dead come about and when will the new world come? He said to them: What you expect has come, but you know it not.

"What you expect *has come*, but you know it not," said Jesus, some 2000 years ago. Cannot this same truth be said *today* to the countless Christian sects that adamantly expect the, so-called, Second Coming? *They know it not.* They expect the kingdom without, not the Kingdom Within. They will have a long wait.[77]

This earth came into being for one reason only. To facilitate and accelerate our learning process by contrast. By the principle of dualism. In a 'goody-goody' world, such as is supposed to happen during the so-called Millennium, dualism would no longer serve any purpose. The earth would not be earth—the realm of becoming. It would be a state of mental and spiritual stagnation. And anyway, according to Jesus, heaven... *has come*. At least some 2000 years ago. It is already here—within us.

Wake up!

***

---

[77]   It might be of some consolation to the Adventists that the Orthodox Jews are also waiting, though they still await the *first* Coming.

52

His disciples said to Him: Twenty-four prophets spoke in Israel and they all spoke about (lit. "in") Thee. He said to them: You have dismissed the Living (One) who is before you and you have spoken about the dead.

We always seem to do that. We ignore that which is before our very noses, and we look further away. We search for truth in India, we visit Israel, the Andean peaks of Machu Picchu, the monasteries, the convents, churches, synagogues, temples. And yet the *only* temple where the *Living One* resides is in our hearts. Surely, it is the shortest journey.

***

53

His disciples said to Him: Is circumcision profitable or not? He said to them: If it were profitable, their father would beget them circumcised from their mother. But the true circumcision in Spirit has become profitable in every way.

"Their father would beget..." Here Jesus attests to the theory of evolution; what He is saying is: "If circumcision was any good to anybody, Mother Nature would have taken care of it by now." Nature deals with our *physical* necessities.

This is not to be confused with the circumcision of Spirit. Webster dictionary defines the *non*-physical circumcision as follows: "rejection of the sins of the flesh; spiritual purification, and acceptance of the Christian faith."

No wonder so many find it easier to chop off a piece of foreskin.

***

54

Jesus said: Blessed are the poor, for yours is the Kingdom of Heaven.

So what's wrong with money? Nothing. What is wrong is the *attachment* to money. Why? *For where your treasure is, there your heart be also.*[78] If we are granted any material assets it is because our Higher Self deems such to be most propitious for our spiritual growth. If we concentrate on the acquisition of money, we detract from our main objective. If money is a *byproduct* of our efforts, by enjoying it, we practice spiritual life.

Anyway, I've never heard of any money 'within'.

And then there is the second meaning.

Jesus taught spiritual truth and therefore the word *poor* must also apply to *the poor in spirit.*[79] Now, this sounds like an oxymoron. How can one be poor when Spirit is the source of all knowledge? The meaning is that he who is prepared to give up all his (present) knowledge in order for the Spirit to fill him (her) with still greater pearls of wisdom, he is truly blessed. There is no end to Spiritual evolution. After all, God is infinite, and we are in Its (His) image. There is likewise no end to our capacity to receive and absorb *new* knowledge.

But we cannot fill old bottles with new wine. (Not if we don't scrub them and sterilize them first!) We must get rid of the old in order to accept the new. *I die daily,*[80] asserts Paul of Taurus, in his readiness to accept *new* dictates of Spirit. Paul not only

---

[78]   Luke 12:34
[79]   Matthew 5:3
[80]   1 Corinthians 15:31

shows evidence of divine wisdom, but seems capable of negating all that constitutes his ego. It is not easy. After all, ego is the sum-total of what we know. It is what our personality is made of.

A man who is poor in Spirit is the richest man of all.

***

55

Jesus said: Whoever does not hate his father and his mother will not be able to be a disciple to Me, and (whoever does not) hate his brethren and his sisters and (does not) take up his cross in My way will not be worthy of Me.

This is a tough one. There are no two measures. It's an all or nothing proposition. Jesus did not teach hatred to one's parents. He taught total detachment from all things material. Our mothers and fathers are our past. Our past is responsible for the mind-set we have so painstakingly created. We became proud of our material possessions, even of our emotional attachments, of our mental or intellectual achievements. Or our... traditions.

Our instruction is simple. Drop it all. All. "Take up your cross and follow me." Sounds tough until we realize that He who advocates this policy is also known as the Prince of Peace (see *logion* 4), and as the personification of Love Itself. Maybe it wouldn't be so hard after all?

If there are still people who associate the cross with suffering, let me add one more quotation: *my yoke is easy and my burden is light.*[81]

So, don't worry...

And also, please read logion 90.

***

---

[81]   Matthew 11:30

56

Jesus said: Whoever has known the world has found a corpse, and whoever has found a corpse, of him the world is not worthy.

One would hope that by repeating the same truth over and over again, sooner or later at least some people would understand the substance of His teaching. Here, once again, Jesus states that the (physical) world we regard as real is no more than a corpse. It is the result and not the cause. On the other hand he who recognizes this truth, who recognizes that the material world is no more than a corpse, an aftermath, a mere shadow of the True Reality, of such a person the world is not worthy.

It may be of some interest to aspiring students of the gospel of Thomas that our modern-day science confirms Jesus' assumptions. The cells of your and my body continue to die even as new ones take their place. Even the atoms of which all things are made have their 'half-life', which places them in a continuous process of disintegration. It would be true to say that our bodies are corpses in a continuous process of recreation.

***

57

Jesus said: The Kingdom of the Father is like a man who had [good] seed. His enemy came by night, he sowed a weed among the good seed. The man did not permit them (the workers) to pull up the weed. He said to them: Lest perhaps you go to pull up* the weed and pull up the wheat with it. For on the day of harvest the weeds will appear, they (will) pull them and burn them.

*(Transl. comment) "to pull up"; lit.: "saying: We will pull up"

This again is a reaffirmation of the two essential truth about ourselves: one, we are immortal (thus there is no hurry), and two, when we shed our physical (emotional and mental) body, we only retain that which becomes the enriching characteristic of the immortal Soul.

Some people find it difficult to locate proof of the philosophy of reincarnation in the Bible. They seem to assume (or perhaps take some biblical passages literally) that God constructed the world in which people will be given a single physical body, do their best with it, and then spend the rest of eternity either being bored in heaven, or suffering torments in hell. The concept of reincarnation was so widely accepted in the past, so obvious to all that had any spiritual training, that the thesis of an eternal heaven and hell made absolutely no sense. There had been no need to state the obvious. There is hardly any need now.

Those who are not yet awakened to their true nature may find this a little unnerving. The concept of infinite life entails infinite responsibility.[82] But we are *all* born to learn of our inherent immor-

---

82   This is another aspect of the concept of karma.

tality. It is up to us to accept it, or... continue to walk in circles until we do.

The comforting lesson in this *logion* is that whatever good seed (spiritual virtues) have been acquired (made part of our consciousness) shall never be lost. Such positive traits became part of that aspect of our nature that is immortal.

***

58

Jesus said: Blessed is the man who has suffered, he has found the Life.

Note: *has* suffered. Past tense. Any person who ever attempted to free him/herself from the insidious attachment to things material, has suffered. To mention a few: overcoming the attachment to smoking, to drinking (excessively), to being a workaholic, attachment to the pursuit of monetary gains... In fact overcoming the attachment to all things, actions, emotions, desires, thoughts, even people—results in suffering. If it doesn't it means that you are blessed. Congratulations. You are already free. You have found Life!

There is a subtle trap set for us on our journey towards freedom. On occasion, we seem to convince ourselves that we shall make spiritual progress by placing allegiance to other *people* rather than to our Higher Self. Members of religious orders may feel such subservience towards their monastic elders; lower army ranks towards their military superiors, employees towards their bosses, and more often than not, wives towards their husbands. There is also a category of people, particularly after periods of armed conflicts (wars), who claim: "I was just carrying out my orders." All such allegiances are wrong. Blaming our own lack of discrimination on others shall never remove our total responsibility for our actions. Neither an army general, nor a priest, nor a rabbi, nor a domineering husband shall assume the blame for *our* misdeeds. We are assured that they will pay their full debt on their own, even as you and I will for listening to them.

Jesus makes it quite clear: No *man can serve two masters.*[83]
This statement applies to any form of duality. We may think that
we shall gain spiritual growth by serving our superiors, our 'spiritual' mentors, our husbands or wives, rather than God. A form of
indirect worship? In doing so, more often than not, all we do is try
to satisfy our own emotional needs.

God is One. The same divine entity resides within all men,
all women. Life of service is a beautiful life, a life with many re-
wards, a life that *can* assure tremendous spiritual progress. And if
we are so advanced as to perceive the Divine Self within our
bosses, our husbands, our wives, all's well. If we are not so advanced, as yet, we would better be sure that we do not *hinder* the
spiritual progress of people we associate with by paying too much
attention to their body, their emotional needs, their stature, social
standing, money or power, or even their minds—rather than the
Spirit which resides within them.

It is not easy.

***

---

[83]   Matthew 6:24

59

Jesus said: Look upon the Living (One) as long as you live, lest you die and seek to see Him and be unable to see.

Whatever spiritual knowledge we do not learn in this life-time, we do not take with us. Only the spiritual traits, qualities, as-pirations, realizations become part of our immortal Self. If we do not latch on to that which is indestructible, we shall not survive our own physical demise.

A powerful warning. It is now, or it could be never. Perhaps it is not clear that Soul is immortal, but we are not. If we do not learn here and now to identify with our Higher Self, we might never do so. This particular life, this incarnation, will have been wasted. What there might be of our personality, devoid of any uni-versal traits, shall be lost forever. Our unresolved traits of character will gravitate towards our 'animal' souls (*nephesh*), and in time shall be reassembled as aspects of a new personality in our future life on earth.

It almost doesn't seem fair. Nothing in such a consciousness will survive, yet all errors will have to be rectified in a future life of that soul which wasted it's previous opportunity. Tough!

***

60

<They saw> a Samaritan carrying a lamb on his way*[1] to
Judea. He said to His disciples: (Why does) this man (carry) the
lamb with him?*[2] They said to Him: In order that he may kill
it an eat it. He said to them: As long as it is alive, he will not eat
it, but (only) if he has killed it and it has become a corpse. They
said: Otherwise he will not be able to do it. He said to them:
You yourselves, seek a place for yourselves in Repose lest you
become a corpse and be eaten.

(Transl. comments): *[1] lit.: **"going"**; *[2] lit.: **"He concerning
(or: around) the lamb"**. The text must be corrupt.

The Samaritan: A man from Samaria: [Samaria (like any
other 'place') symbolizes a particular state of consciousness. In
Hebrew the word *Samaria* means: *watch, guard, lookout,* (Greek
equivalent: of Shomron: meaning *guard*)]. A Samaritan would
therefore be a man enjoying a particular state of consciousness.

Judea: once again, being 'land', a place one resides in, implies a specific state of consciousness; In Hebrew the word Judah
means: praised.

The lambs: symbolize thoughts, particularly *spiritual ideas.*

To kill: to *deprive of spiritual content.*

To eat it: to *absorb it, to make it part of your nature.*

A place: a *state of consciousness.*

Repose: *the Sabbath, the Spiritual consciousness.*[84]

These are mostly 'mental' equivalents of the words and their
symbolic meaning. Try your own hand at an interpretation. Finding

---

[84]   Refer to DICTIONARY OF BIBLICAL SYMBOLISM by the
author of the Commentary

your own spiritual meaning within the Scriptures is worth more than reading a thousand books of other people's conclusions. He, who does not seek, is very unlikely to find the real meaning, especially the meaning that applies to that particular person, at his or her particular stage of the journey.

A personal note:

Relying on other peoples' interpretation does not really advance you. After all, our *perception* of Truth or Reality changes with each step of our evolution. We all travel our own paths, at our own pace.

***

61

Jesus said: Two will rest on a bed: the one will die, the one will live. Salome said: Who art thou, man, and whose (son)?* Thou didst take thy place upon my bench and eat from my table. Jesus said to her: I am He who is from the Same, to Me was given from the things of My Father. <Salome said>: I am Thy disciple. <Jesus said to her>: Therefore I say, if he is the Same, he will be filled with light, but if he is divided, he will be filled with darkness.

(Transl. comment)   Lit.: **as from whom.** Ms.: **as from somebody.**

This is a form of contemplation.

I would suggest that Thomas took it out of the context and thus made it enigmatic. The apparent conversation appears to be between Jesus' higher and lower nature. Salome means *perfect* or *peace*, from Hebrew shalôm: wellbeing. In this context Salome is inquiring into the state of consciousness of Jesus' Higher Self. We must realize that no matter how advanced we may be on the path of spiritual evolution, for as long as we are on this earth, the lower self must be present to assure physical survival. That is why on one occasion Jesus remonstrated with a disciple who addressed Him as the Good Master. Jesus replied: Why *callest thou me good? There is none good but one, that is, God.*[85] He was attempting to explain to the disciple that as long as we live in a dual world, the balance between 'good' and 'bad' must be maintained.

The terms are, of course, relative.

To get back to the *logion*.

---

[85]   Mark 10:17-18

Jesus illustrates the duality of man's psyche: the *Is* and the *Ra*, the male and the female principles.[86] The two aspects of man's nature shall enter a state of Repose ("rest on a bed"). One (conscious awareness) will die, while the soul (*nephesh* or the subconscious) will continue (live on, or continue to function). It should be mentioned that by the subconscious we recognize the sum-total of our accumulated experience. It is that state of consciousness that we have acquired through constant repetition of thoughts, emotions, and actions. In this case this lower soul, *nephesh*, is represented by Salome. Comparing to the struggles of everyday conscious experiences, the subconscious, the accumulated 'goodness', is a state of peace.

Salome (the subconscious) is aware of a different Entity invading its awareness. It inquires into Its identity: "Who art thou? Are you a man, and if so, from whom are you" (meaning are you born of a woman, or of Spirit). Then Salome recognizes previous encounters with the Higher Self. She says: "You have made yourself known to me before, in fact, you have drawn from my offerings".

Jesus, now speaking as the Higher Self, replies: "I am He who is from the Single Source (the Same). I am the Spirit."

Salome (already the center of wellbeing) recognizes her own Higher Nature. She confesses that she is Its (His) disciple.[87]

Jesus instructs Salome (or more precisely us) how to recognize her own Higher Self. If He is who He says He is, then He is no longer of a divided consciousness (i.e.: of the world of duality). And if that is so, than He must be filled with Divine Knowledge (Light). But if he is divided, i.e.: judgmental, if he is not beyond the duality of 'good and evil', than he still has not achieved divine knowledge. Essentially Jesus teaches us that the Higher Self is the

---

[86] See commentary to *logion 30*

[87] When referring to Higher Self, the scriptures invariably use the masculine form (Father, Lord, Master) because it symbolizes the conscious as against the subconscious awareness. This distinction has nothing to do with the 'physical' sexual orientation. As the reader must be aware, the Higher Self is Spirit, neither male nor female, yet possessed of both qualities in Its infinite potential.

Source of All. Of everything. That nothing exists outside the reality of Spirit. That any other approach is filled with darkness.

Or to put it even more succinctly: God is One.

***

62

Jesus said: I tell My mysteries to those [who are worthy of my] mysteries. What thy right (hand) will do, let not thy left (hand) know what it does.

It is paradoxical that even assuming that my commentary is an acceptable explanation of the 'mysteries', the readers who are not 'ready' to receive them, shall not do so. The mystery will remain a mystery protected not by the symbolic, enigmatic, or esoteric language, but by the state of consciousness of the reader.

I repeat the words of Thomas Aquinas I included in my comments to *logion* 33: *Whatever is received is received according to the nature of the recipient.*

To those who wish to take the risk of understanding (or being hopelessly confused by my comments!), the right hand symbolizes the executive, masculine or the conscious (*Ra*) aspect of our nature, and the left hand the passive, feminine or the subconscious (*Is*). The reason for this strange admonition is that the positive mind receives its input directly from Spirit i.e.: the executive is inspired by the intuitive, while the subconscious (soul) is the stockpile of accumulated experience normally referred to as instinct. The latter is often concerned with knowledge necessary for physical survival. As such, it is of no interest to Jesus.

***

63

Jesus said: There was a rich man who had much money. He said: I will use my money that I may sow and reap and plant and fill my storehouses with fruit, so that I lack nothing. This was what he thought in his heart. And that night he died. Whoever has ears let him hear.

We are discouraged from postponing living till later. We are advised to live in the present.

I knew a man who had forty-three million dollars. He committed suicide. He was bored.

***

64

Jesus said: A man had guest-friends, and when he had prepared the dinner, he sent his servant to invite the guest-friends.
He went to the first, he said to him: "My master invites thee".
He said: "I have some claims against some merchants; they will
come to me in the evening; I will go and give them my orders. I
pray to be excused from the dinner". He went to another, he
said to him: "My master has invited thee". He said to him: "I
have bought a house and they request me for a day. I will have
no time". He came to another, he said to him: "My master invites thee". He said to him: "My friend is to be married and I
am to arrange a dinner; I shall not be able to come. I pray to be
excused from the dinner". He went to another, he said to him:
"My master invites thee". He said to him: "I have bought a
farm, I go to collect the rent. I shall not be able to come. I pray
to be excused".

The servant came, he said to his master: "Those whom
thou hast invited to the dinner have excused themselves". The
master said to his servant: "Go out to the roads, bring those
whom thou shalt find, so that they may dine. Tradesmen and
merchants [shall] not [enter] the places of my Father".

This is an elaboration of the previous *logion*. It is sadly apparent how grave difficulties people had in understanding Jesus'
words.

I've met so many people who said that spiritual interests are
all right once you're old and gray, but surely, there are better things
to do while we are in full command of our bodies (probably meaning minds). Time enough later, they said.

Not everyone has a 'later'. Like the rich man, some die before reaching an old age. Some live longer but they forget why. Some remember, vaguely, but... have trouble concentrating.

Some might not get invited—later.

***

65

**He said: A good man had a vineyard. He gave it to husband-
men so that they would work it and that he would receive its
fruit from them. He sent his servant so that the husbandmen
would give him the fruit of the vineyard. They seized his servant, they beat him; a little longer and they would have killed
him. The servant came, he told it to this master. His master
said: "Perhaps he did not know them"*. He sent another servant; the husbandmen beat him as well. Then the owner sent
his son. He said: "Perhaps they will respect my son." Since
those husbandmen knew that he was the heir of the vineyard,
they seized him, they killed him. Whoever has ears let him
hear.**

*(Translator's comment): read: **"perhaps they did not recognize him"**

Here Jesus predicts His own death.

In case there is any doubt as to the meaning of the *logion*:

A good man is God. The vineyard is His Kingdom. We are
the husbandmen. The servants are the prophets. The son is the Son.

***

66

Jesus said: Show me the stone which the builders have rejected; it is the corner-stone.

We are the builders of the Temple. The Temple is to be in our heart. The Temple can only be built in a state of consciousness exhibiting peace. A state of absolute detachment. Such a serene state of consciousness is always symbolized in the Bible by the City of Jerusalem. It has nothing whatever to do with a pile of stone, brick and mortar which those who interpret the Bible literally would like to see rebuilt in the State of Israel. Nothing at all.

Jesus talks about the premise on which you base your state of consciousness. We always seem to reject the premises that are the most important, the corner-stones. After all, the basic premise must be that we are not physical but spiritual beings. That we are in but not of this world.[88] That our kingdom is also not of this world. These are the corner-stones we tend to reject. The problem is that the corner-stone is invariably so intangible. It is up to us to make it real.

***

---

[88]   John 8:23, 15:19, 17:14, 17:16 et al.

67

Jesus said: Whoever knows the All but fails (to know) himself lacks everything.

It is evident that there is only one way to know God and that is by finding Him within our own heart. He, who fails in doing so, will never find Him anywhere else.[89]

***

---

[89]   A point of interest: some four hundred years before Jesus walked the earth, Socrates (469-399 B.C.), who also paid with his life for his beliefs, advocated his followers to know themselves. Later he added that "An unexamined life is not worth living." Echoes of the future?

68

Jesus said: Blessed are you when you are hated and persecuted; and no place will be found there where you have been persecuted.*

*(Transl. comment): read: **"you will find a place, where you will not be persecuted".**[90]

We are to become independent of any external influences. The place where we are hated and persecuted is within our own minds. Within whatever we perceive as our reality. And thus, we are hated and persecuted by our own negative thoughts; by our lower nature, our attachments, our weaknesses, and most of all by our ego. We, and only we, are responsible for our suffering.

When we become aware of these enemies, these hateful thoughts, we are blessed, for we have taken the first step towards that reality wherein nothing can touch us, nothing can persecute us, where we shall reign as Princes within our own Kingdom.

***

---

[90]   Thomas O. Lambdin in the Nag Hammadi Library publication translates the second phrase of the *legion* as follows: "Wherever you have been persecuted they will find no place." The writer prefers the version offered by the "Translator's comment".

69a

Jesus said: Blessed are those who have been persecuted in their heart; these are they who have known the Father in truth.

This *logion*, the preceding one, and the one that follows, all teach the same truth.

In all three Jesus elaborates the postulate that once we have started the battle in our hearts, in our consciousness, we have already become aware of our Higher Self. Aware of Him who is our Father. It may be still a very rudimentary realization, one barely skirting the periphery of our awareness, but, at long last, we are on the way.

***

69b

Blessed are the hungry, for the belly of him who desires will be filled.*
*(Transl. comment) possibly: "they will fill their belly with what they desire".

As always, it is the spiritual hunger, and the spiritual 'belly' that shall be sated. If the translator's comment (alternative translation) is correct, then the *logion* states that we decide what shall constitute our consciousness. It must be very important therefore to assure that the desires we hold are such that their fulfillment shall bring us permanent joy.

***

70

Jesus said: If you bring forth that within yourselves, that which you have will save you. If you do not have that within yourselves, that which you do not have within you will kill you.

A frightening thought. That which is within us is, of course, our Higher Self. The first part of the *logion* is obvious. The second part is the frightening one, yet it only repeats what had been said before. The absence of the divine is paramount to death. Spiritual death—to Jesus there is none other.

The Higher Self dwells within everyone, of course. However, we, the puny humans are possessed of free will. Whatever we refuse to accept as reality does not become part of our subjective reality. *According to your faith be it unto you.*[91] The Law cannot be broken. That which we refuse to recognize will remain absent. The absence of Life is death. It is our choice. A frightening thought.

It could be as though we haven't lived at all.

***

---

[91]   Matthew 9:29

71

Jesus said: I shall de[stroy this] house and no one will be able to build it [again].

Every consciousness is an individualized expression of God. Jesus recognizes that it is only with His acquiescence that His 'house', His state of consciousness can be destroyed. Every 'house' is unique. None can be built again. None can be duplicated.

To the Adventist this *logion* carries a sad message. Jesus states that this is His last reincarnation. His state of consciousness shall never walk this earth again.

Those who are at odds with His, so called, Second Coming needn't worry. Jesus, having achieved unity with His (and our) Father, is present in every one of us as the Higher Self. It is up to us, of course, to realize it. Or, to make His presence, or His nature, real within our consciousness.[92]

This can only be achieved in spirit.

***

---

[92]   I am of the opinion that the sum total of His individuality remains indestructible in higher realms of which some mystics speak....

72

[A man said] to Him: Tell my brethren to divide my father's possessions with me. He said to him: O man, who made Me (a) divider? He turned to His disciples, he said to them: I am not a divider, am I?

Once again Jesus reiterates that He is not interested in worldly matters. It is wonderful to note that the most advanced Consciousness that ever walked this earth is not immune to a sense of humor! One can only speculate at the expression on His face when, turning to his disciples He asked: "I am not a divider, am I?"

There is, however, a lesson attached to this *logion*. And the lesson is that whosoever we are, no matter what our function or mission in life, no matter how 'important' we are—or think we are, we are not to take ourselves too seriously.

On a more serious note, Jesus' whole teaching is directed at the unification of the male and female principles through the intercession of *'El'*, the unifying principle or our High Self. To become whole, we must become one.

***

73

Jesus said: The harvest is indeed great, but the labourers are few; but beg the Lord to send labourers into the harvest.

As so often in esoteric writings, there are two meanings inherent in this *logion*. First: we are the harvest while the saints, the prophets, the saviors are the laborers.

The second meaning is more important.

We must never loose track that Jesus always taught on a one-on-one basis. Each soul is an entire universe, a potential Kingdom, a haven for Divine Presence. No matter what the lesson, it is only as good as it applies to a single soul, a single seeker. So few lessons get through to us. It is the seeker who determines the validity of the lesson. We cannot receive, let alone metabolize, what we cannot understand.

Ultimately, we are to become independent of any and all external influences; even the 'good' influences of souls more advanced than we are. We must stop relying on external influences such as priesthood, preachers, books or even scriptures, and rely *solely* on spiritual input from within. For this input, these 'laborers', we are to beg the Lord. It is as much a prayer for the message as for our understanding. By prayer, I mean a contemplative attitude that facilitates such contact. Only such (eventual) approach can result in freedom that will lead us to becoming kings within our own kingdoms.

In this context, the harvest symbolizes the constant stream of thoughts which race through our consciousness. Regardless what we do or do not do, the turbulent oceans of our minds appear to sway us in this and that direction; we often find ourselves without a rudder, without a captain at the helm. Only occasional, momentary inspirations lead us back in the right direction, fill our sails with new will and desire to maintain a firm, if still inexperienced, hold on our destinies. Once again, it is for those inspirations, those fleeting visions that we beg the Lord, that those moments of enlightenment might be multiplied and keep us on an even keel.

The Lord is, of course, the I AM, our High Self, the Divine Presence within us.

It is my contention that the 'word' is always flowing. It is our listening that is blocked.

***

74

He said: Lord, there are many around the cistern, but nobody in the cistern.

A cistern is a container for water, and water in the Scriptures invariably symbolizes the human soul, the psyche, as represented by the mental movement, i.e.: that in which a change of consciousness takes place.[93] The sum-total of this psyche is also symbolized by our feminine, or passive nature. In order for a change to occur, the psyche must be imbued, or infused, with *conscious* awareness. In the Scriptures the male, positive aspect of our nature symbolizes this awareness.

We should never loose track that Jesus had been teaching most advanced concepts of psychology using whatever images had been available to Him in His time. The 'woman', as representing the psyche, must not be confused with a female-human-being as against a male-human-being. While there are certain differences between men's and women's psyches, both are possessed of similar psychological structures, both enjoy (or fail to do so) their conscious and subconscious to the degree of their spiritual advancement. Many religions appear to have forgotten that the purpose of a symbol is to illustrate a concept and not to have it supplant the truth that it represents. It is a means to an end, never an end in itself.

By entering the cistern, we unify the male and female principle within us.

***

---

[93]   Kapuscinski, S. DICTIONARY OF BIBLICAL SYMBOLISM

75

Jesus said: Many are standing at the door, but the solitary are the ones who will enter the bridal chamber.

The Gnostic Gospel of Philip defines the bridal chamber as follows: *"A bridal chamber is not for the animals, nor is it for the slaves, nor for defiled women; but it is for free men and virgins."*[94] Later the writer of the Gospel of Philip refers to the bridal Chamber as *"the holy of the holies."* It is indeed a most exalted state of consciousness.

The door, gates etc, symbolize a *change* in consciousness resulting in new understanding. Thus many are on the brink of such a change, on the brink of gaining a new (spiritual) understanding, but few will enter the bridal chamber. The latter symbol defines a state of consciousness where the two become one. It is a condition of unification, wherein the male and the female aspects of our nature, or the conscious and the subconscious, the active and the passive (or reactive), become one. We eliminate duality. According to the *Gospel of Philip,* to achieve this condition we must be fully aware of our spiritual nature. We must no longer be slaves to any preconceived ideas. Our subconscious mind must be rid of any negativity. We must be free of any attachments; we must be born of Spirit and remain faithful to It. Then, and only then we can enter the bridal chamber.

This is the process of salvation. To be saved means to realign our subconscious, our (animal) soul,[95] with that which we receive or attain through conscious understanding of the nature of our

---

[94]   NAG HAMMADI LIBRARY: The Gospel of Philip (pg.151) as translated by Wesley W. Isenberg.
[95]   Which defines our personality.

Higher Self. It is a long and arduous process. It may have taken countless generations to develop our present mind-set, yet, we are told to change our assumptions, to reject all that we hold 'holy', to give up our most cherished ideas. Paul the apostle had defined this process of giving up in his statement: *I die daily.*[96] He'd meant that at all times he had been ready to give up all his beliefs in order to accept the dictates of Spirit, of Higher Self.

Jesus put it differently: The *wind bloweth where it listeth, and thou hearest the sound thereof, but canst not tell whence it cometh, and whither it goeth: so is every one that is born of the Spirit.*[97] Everyone. It is an incredible assertion that even he (or, perhaps, particularly he) who is possessed of Christ Consciousness does not know from one moment to another where, how and to what end will the Spirit use him.

Yet so many of us so often claim that we already know at least some of the answers.

Jesus said that He did not know. He had to listen to the Spirit.[98]

***

---

[96]   1 Corinthians 15:31

[97]   John 3:8. The wind is a translation of the Greek word *pneuma*, meaning breath or spirit.

[98]   Remember Socrates? He is said to have said, "I know that I know nothing". It seems that he knew a great deal...

76

Jesus said: The Kingdom of the Father is like a man, a merchant, who possessed merchandise (and) found a pearl. That merchant was prudent. He sold the merchandise, he bought the one pearl for himself. Do you also seek for the treasure which fails not, which endures, there where no moth comes near to devour and (where) no worm destroys.

See *logion* 8.

We are the merchants, the wise fishermen. Jesus claims that all we possess is worth giving up, selling, if we could but find that one, singular pearl. A pearl, which cannot be destroyed, an incorruptible treasure. If your or my broker told us that he knows of an investment that cannot lose. That it is guarantied—unconditionally—forever. Would we not buy it?

Jesus is making us such an offer. Only, please note. The investment cannot be made for someone else. You can only buy the pearl for *yourself*. Thank God there are enough pearls to go around.

Yet... in a very strange way, the pearl is only One.

***

77

Jesus said: I am the Light that is above them all, I am the All, the All come forth from Me and the All attained to Me. Cleave a (piece of) wood, I am there; lift up the stone and you will find Me there.

If I ascend up into heaven, thou art there: if I make my bed in hell, behold, thou art there. If I take the wings of the morning, and dwell in the uttermost parts of the sea even there shall thy hand lead me, and thy right hand shall hold me...[99]   The psalmist goes on.

This is Christ Consciousness speaking. It is a magnificent assurance of the omnipresence of the Divine. It is also an affirmation of the One God. Nothing exists outside or beyond the concept of God. God is All and All ensues from God.[100] And God finds Its expression through us. Through you and me.

Ye are gods.[101]

Scary? Sublime? Ineffable?

***

---

[99]   Psalm 139:8-9 et all.

[100]   In Bhagavad-Gita, Krishna puts it this way, "I am the source of everything. From Me the entire creation flows. Knowing this, the wise worship Me with all their hearts." [Translation by A.C. Bhaktivedanta Swami Prabhupada, Chapter 10, verse 8]. Another translator, Sir Edwin Arnold waxes poetic the same verse "Yea! Knowing Me the source of all, by Me all creatures wrought, The wise in spirit cleave to Me, into My Being brought."

[101]   Psalm 82:6, John 10:34

78

Jesus said: Why did you come out into the desert? To see a reed shaken by the wind? And to see a man clothed in soft garments? [See, your] kings and your great ones are those who are clothed in soft [garments] and they [shall] not be able to know the truth.

Jesus is talking about John the Baptist. For elaboration of the theme see Matthew chapter 11, verses 1 - 15.

***

79

**A woman from the multitude said to Him: Blessed is the womb
which bore Thee and the breasts which nourished Thee. He
said to [her]: Blessed are those who have heard the word of the
Father (and) have kept it in truth. For there will be days when
you will say: Blessed is the womb which has not conceived and
the breasts which have not suckled.**

The Father—as usual: the Higher Self; the Spirit imbued
with self-awareness. He who hears the voice of the Father is he
who is born of Spirit, born of the womb that has *not* conceived. It
may be of interest to the readers that in esoteric writings, the Spirit
had been almost invariably portrayed as female (i.e. implying the
static, sustaining condition of being, as against the state of becoming).

It could not have been easy for Jesus to convey the concept
of Spiritual birth. It seems quite difficult even today.

***

80

Jesus said: Whoever has known the world has found the body, and whoever has found the body, of him the world is not worthy.

If Jesus wanted to confuse us, He couldn't have put it better!

I shall attempt to decipher the riddle. The *world* or the *earth* normally symbolizes physical awareness. The *body*, on the other hand, stands for the individualization of Soul. It is that which makes us different from one another. Ultimately, the only body we shall be aware of will be the soul body, the spiritualized body, the Higher Self. We can think of our immortal body (Soul) to be made up of Spirit, our mortal soul, or our subconscious (the Biblical *nephesh*)[102] to be made up of thoughts (or thought patterns), and our material body of 'physical' atoms.

He, therefore, who became aware of his physical consciousness, became aware of his individualized existence. He became aware of his uniqueness. Although this is no more than the first step, by taking it we enter on the search for our true identity. Once we do so, we step beyond the merely physical consciousness, we *per force* progress to higher states, become aware that there is more to us than just the 'world'.

***

---

[102] YOUNG'S ANALYTICAL CONCORDANCE TO THE BIBLE pg. 917

81

Jesus said: Let him who has become rich become king, and let him who has power renounce (it).

A truly beautiful *logion*.

The richness is, of course, spiritual wealth. It is the indestructible richness of Spirit that fills our soul to overflowing. I am reminded of the psalmist crying out: *my cup runneth over.*[103] It is a feeling, an experience, of abundance beyond words. He who is that rich, let him become king. Let him rule in his kingdom because from such a realm he can hand out riches to all who visit him.

And now the warning.

Such an enormous wealth carries equally enormous power. Power of life and death, power over all the lower states of consciousness.[104] Not only one's own but other peoples', particularly those who have not yet risen to their own full potential. People who only just tasted those powers tend to experiment with them. They can hurt, even destroy, those possessed of lower states of awareness. Such an act is a great spiritual crime carrying very exacting karma.[105] Such power must be immediately renounced.

There is one further collateral to this *logion*.

Those who have dared to venture into the higher states of consciousness, into the worlds of Spirit, make a claim that will

---

[103]   Psalm 23:5

[104]   The mental, emotional and physical states.

[105]   The subject of *karma* is too vast to discuss here in detail. Suffice it to say that it is a spiritual law exemplified in and by the so-called 'golden rule'. It is wise to remember that the law covers our physical, emotional and mental behavior. It is the immutable law of retribution.

hearten all travelers on their spiritual journey. Those intrepid travelers say that once we cross the great divide between the worlds of matter and the realm of Spirit, one no longer finds power.

There, beyond that intangible chasm, within the True Reality, we shall find only Love.

***

82

Jesus said: Whoever is near to me is near to the fire, and whoever is far from me is far from the Kingdom.

Fire, almost invariably symbolizes a cleansing process. The Kingdom can only be entered through a single door. Through and by the recognition of the divinity within. No one can do it for us. Not even the Man many refer to as the Savior. What the Savior had done was to show us the Way. We must cross the threshold ourselves.

Whoever decides to enter the Kingdom must cleanse himself of all attachments, of his or her lower nature. Jesus compares himself to the cleansing fire. He also says that unless we undergo this purification of our consciousness, we shall remain far from the Kingdom.

***

83

Jesus said: The images are manifest to man and the Light which is within them is hidden in the Image of the Light of the Father. He will manifest himself and His Image is concealed by His Light.

We cannot see the Face of God. We could never encompass such an Image of the Infinite. No stretch of the imagination, no power of the mind can reveal the enormity of the concept of the Whole. No matter how high we rise, we shall only know God through the Spiritual Knowledge that radiates from Its throne.

As individualizations, we are finite. The finite cannot comprehend that which is Infinite. But we can observe Its Light. It is manifest in Love, Beauty, Serenity, Harmony, in the simplicity of the wild flower, in a song of a nightingale, in the majesty of the mountains, in the firmament filled with stars, nebulas and galaxies. We can also perceive Its Presence in the eyes of a newborn baby.

***

84

Jesus said: When you see your likeness, you rejoice. But when you see your images which came into existence before you, (which) neither die nor are manifested, how much will you bear!*

*(Transl. comment) Exclamation or question.

Your likeness is the perception of who you really are. Your awareness that there is more to you than meets the eye. But then, in time, you realize that all the positive traits which you have developed in your past lives have become part of your wealth. Those traits cannot die, cannot cease to be nor, in the strictest sense of the word, are they manifested. Why? Because in your present life your task is to acquire new traits. The attributes we had already acquired we tend to take for granted. No man seems able to fully appreciate his ability to walk or read or write or even think logically, unless placed in opposition to one who cannot perform these tasks. Only then such shortcomings become apparent.

But there are moments when we become aware of the magnitude of the journey we have already traveled. Of the battles we have fought and won. We become aware of our previous lives, previous incarnations. We regard ourselves from the point of view of our immortal Self. These are moments of our own, secret, personal joy and glory. How much joy can one bear!

***

85

Jesus said: Adam came into existence from a great power and a great wealth, and (yet) he did not become worthy of you. For if he had been worthy, [he would] not [have tasted] death.

The pinnacle of evolution is a physical (material) construct that is capable of receiving and giving expression to a single unit (entity) of self-conscious awareness. Such a construct is Adam. This allegorical man symbolizes a state of consciousness that identifies itself with the physical body. It is possessed, nevertheless, of self-awareness. It can state with pride: 'I am', even if that which he thinks he is remains transient, perishable. Thus Adam died. Adam had chosen duality over wholeness. This is the meaning of the parable of the tree of knowledge. No part of his personality survived to be reincarnated into future cycles.

Only that which identifies itself with the immortal can become immortal. The first such 'person' which became aware of his spiritual nature is symbolized by Jacob.[106] He, Jacob, is the prototype of a more advanced state of consciousness. It must be stressed that every 'person' in esoteric teachings represents a unit of self-awareness. Thus Jacob, still a primitive man, nevertheless is an entity *aware of his spiritual nature.* As such, there will be fragments of Jacob's personality that will survive. The positive traits, though still primitive, but worth preserving. They will grow and develop in future embodiments.

A man called Israel symbolizes the next step on the evolutionary scale. Jacob is renamed Israel when he becomes fully aware of his *divine* nature. In the Bible, an Israelite symbolizes any soul that is actively seeking God. (We already know from previous *lo-*

---

[106]   refer to the DICTIONARY OF BIBLICAL SYMBOLISM

gia that we can only seek divinity *within* our own consciousness). Such a person is apt to develop traits that become immortal. These traits become metabolized by the soul.[107] Thus as the soul continues to be spiritualized, or sanctified, it eventually becomes immortal. It begins its long process of assimilation into its Higher Self. Ultimately it becomes the King in Its own, immortal, indestructible Kingdom.

One cannot but wonder how many 'Adams' are still roaming the world today. They have a long journey ahead. They all need help from those who have already become as *James the righteous for whose sake heaven and earth came into being.*[108]

***

---

[107]   Once again, 'soul' translated from Hebrew *nephesh* means the animal soul, or the subconscious, which symbolizes the storehouse of knowledge necessary for our physical survival. By spiritualizing it, we assure the survival of our individuality.

[108]   see *logion* 12

86

Jesus said: [The foxes] [have] the[ir holes] and the birds have [their] nest, but the Son of Man has no place to lay his head and to rest.

All students of the Bible know this *logion* from the gospels of Matthew and Luke. It invokes in us, perhaps, certain guilt that we have so much while Jesus had so little. Well, our guilt is not warranted.

Jesus is referring once again to the state of being. This time His own. He points out that all who are of this earth, of a physical consciousness, even animals and birds, feel at home on earth. It is a place they call their own. It is their hole, their nest, their home. But Jesus was in this world but not of it.[109] He was the ultimate displaced person. He would not go back to His own Country until He fulfilled His mission. Until then, He would have no place to lay his head and to rest.

***

---

[109]   John 17:14 et al.

87

Jesus said: Wretched is the body which depends upon a body, and wretched is the soul which depends upon these two.

Another allegory.

The body is that which gives us our personality. It is also that which sets us apart. Yet it makes us sad, wretched, to rely on that which separates us. It is indeed sad that all our material bodies: our physical, emotional, mental states of consciousness set us apart. In fact, it is this sense of alienation that we have to overcome.

Jesus singles out the worst condition: one in which we rely exclusively on our physical consciousness and on our separateness. If we rely on that which makes us different—we are bound to end up wretched. We are much better off to dwell on that which unites us, on that which we can share. On that which, ultimately, shall make us One.

***

88

Jesus said: The angels* and the prophets will come to you and they will give you what is yours. And you, too, give to them what is in your hands, and say to yourselves: "On which day will they come and receive what is theirs?"

*(Transl. comments) **"The angels"**, or: **"The messengers"**

A moment of contemplation.

The angels and prophets are all messengers of God. They are advanced souls who overcame their limitations and became co-workers with the One. They bring us that which is ours, which is our heritage. They give us the knowledge how to free ourselves from our self imposed limitations. They give us Light.

I wonder how often we realize that every single one of us had been created for the sole purpose of being saved, i.e. to achieve immortality. Some people seem to think that we are all immortal. Not so. Not according to Jesus. Some he'd called dead.[110] Spiritually dead. Yet we are repeatedly given chances. The whole universe had been created for the sole purpose of advancing our education.[111] Our physical consciousness steeped in a dualistic world enables us to see the consequences of our erroneous thinking almost immediately. If we miss the mark,[112] we see the corollaries, the ramifications in short order. Furthermore, if we chose to ignore the lessons, then each succeeding instruction becomes more persuasive:

...first we feel tired more quickly, perhaps a little shortness of breath, then there might be a certain dryness in the back of the

---

[110]   "Let the dead bury the dead" Matthew 8:22.

[111]   refer to *logion* 12

[112]   see *logion* 14

throat followed by a certain annoying roughness... we clear our throat more often—apparently for no reason, then we might develop a little cough, later—perhaps much later—a bronchitis, then... chronic bronchitis with associated sleeping problems, perhaps emphysema, cardiac and circulatory problems, finally— cancer of the throat or lungs...

We seldom recognize our messengers.

And the funny thing is that it is of absolutely no consequence whether we smoke or not. What matters is that we become attached to that which is purely physical. We rely on other than spiritual remedies, on other than that which is our true nature.

And *On which day will they come and receive what is theirs?* We have the power; it is in our hands, to give them what is theirs. Instead of killing our prophets, crucifying our saviors, ignoring the messengers we might, just might... one day give them their due. Give them love and praise. Give them our gratitude. But most of all, we might one day begin to listen.

***

89

Jesus said: Why do you wash the outside of the cup? Do you not understand that he who made the inside is also he who made the outside?

The outside of the cup symbolizes the outer sheaths of the Soul: the mental, emotional and physical bodies. If we look after the 'inside' of the cup, the outside will take care of itself.

The second meaning is even more interesting.

It implies that all things are made of spirit. There is no real duality. There is no quintessential difference between spirit and matter.[113]

God is One. All is One.

***

---

[113] It might help the reader to think of ice, water and steam. Quintessentially, they are all the same.

90

Jesus said: Come to Me, for easy is My yoke and My lordship is gentle, and you shall find repose for yourselves.

So says the Prince of Peace, the one called Love Incarnate.

Perhaps we can trust Him?

It may be of interest that the reining Pope, the one accused by so many of being inflexible, ultra-orthodox and old-fashioned, entitled his own book of questions and answers: *"Be not afraid."* Can we trust anyone?

Or are we afraid?

***

91

They said to Him: Tell us who Thou art so that we may believe in Thee. He said to them: You test the face of the sky and of the earth, and him who is before your face you have not known, and you do not know to test this moment.

You test the face of the sky and the earth...

We all seem to rely on 'hard' evidence. If we cannot touch it or smell it, or measure it under controlled laboratory conditions, we prefer not to accept it. Or, at the very least, to reserve our judgment. How many of those skeptics, those illustrious scientists of the last 2000 years measured the intensity of love? How many defined the beauty of a flower? How many of them had proven beyond a reasonable doubt that Mozart is more sublime than Beethoven, or perhaps, the other way round? How many of them managed, with their millions of dollars supplied by the governments of the world, to work out, precisely, what a baby feels for her mother––and the mother for her baby?

The disciples could only *test the moment*, could only grasp the moment of infinity, recognize that which is spiritual—with their soul. One cannot measure mind with emotions, emotions with physical senses, nor can one measure spirit with that which is not spiritual. They did not know how to do it.

Do we?

***

92

Jesus said: Seek and you will find, but those things which you asked me in those days, I did not tell you then; now I desire to tell them, but you do not inquire after them.

Jesus knew all his disciples before they entered their present incarnation. Even before descending for yet another stint in the material world, they had already reached a relatively advanced state of consciousness. They had been anxious to learn the Truth. It appears, however, that we can only gather *new* knowledge while on earth. Why? Because we are not to discard our physical consciousness but to sanctify it. If we are to be gods we must conquer *all* the universes, all the states of consciousness. From the most coarse to the most refined. How else could we help other, less advanced souls when it becomes our turn to do so?

And now, you do not inquire after them. After 'things' concerning inner knowledge. They had been so willing, so interested, until other more mundane 'things' got in the way. The 'things' of spirit had to wait.

Does this remind you of anyone?

***

93

<Jesus said:> Give not what is holy to the dogs, lest they cast it on the dung-heap. Throw not the pearls to the swine, lest they make it [......].

See the commentary to *logion* 33.

Secret knowledge is secret because the consciousness of the prospective recipient is not as yet ready to receive it. The intricacies of a fuel injection system would leave little impression on a man living in a jungle. In fact, they would be lost on most of us living in a city. Consciousness must walk its own narrow, often precipitous path, learn at its own pace, absorb knowledge at its own unique rate. There is no hurry, we are immortal.

The warning is particularly addressed to those who wish to impose esoteric knowledge by force. One is reminded of the old crusaders. We are told that: "I will convert you even if it kills you," is not the right attitude.

I am reminded of a Buddhist disciple who had been told to love his enemies. Alas, the acolyte had no enemies. Thus he walked up to the first man he met on the street and hit him in the face. He needed an enemy to love.

***

94

Jesus [said]: Whoever seeks will find [and whoever knocks], it will be opened to him.

This sentiment, this truth, is repeated in all Scriptures. It is truly amazing how few of us take advantage of this assurance. Perhaps some of us are not, as yet, ready. Perhaps some of us are knocking at the wrong door.

Yet we must knock. Repeatedly.

Talking to people, I'd often heard them say that one can learn a great deal from various books. That's true, in a way. It depends also on what knowledge we are seeking.

Nevertheless, this is not Jesus' way. The door we are to knock on is the door leading to our inner self. In the Bible, a door invariably symbolizes a change of consciousness that will lead to and result in new understanding. All knowledge *must* always come from within. It is there, in our inner sanctum, that the true Teacher resides. It is there that we shall eventually discover our kingdom. It is there and only there that our own true Self is waiting to be discovered.

Books have their place, but from the spiritual point of view they serve only to *confirm* that which we already know. Sometimes, when we discover a new, inner truth, we doubt its veracity. It seems so different from all that we've heard people say—all around us. It seems at odds with the universe we live in. That's a good sign,[114] but—the discovery often makes us a little afraid, or at the very least, a little anxious. On occasion, we also feel somewhat lonely. We experience self-doubts. Perhaps, we think, it is our

---

[114]   In fact this is an unequivocal telltale sign.

pride, which makes us think that we are right. How can we be right when everyone says otherwise? How can such a truth not be obvious to everyone? We seem to forget that a short while ago we too had been unaware of its existence.

And this is where books come in.

So often when we discover within a new, heretofore esoteric knowledge, and we experience moments of doubt about its veracity, a book falls into our hands, seemingly by accident, quite unexpectedly. We discover that we are not alone, that somewhere in the world there is someone who also thinks differently—yet, quite like us. Suddenly we know that we no longer have to doubt our personal revelation. We smile at the thought that only a few years ago people said that man would never fly, that the moon is made of cheese, and that the sun spins round the earth. We rediscover that all knowledge *always* comes from within, that we can trust our intuition.

And then we realize, yet again, that someone had already promulgated an identical concept—some 2000 years ago. Someone had said that if we knock it *shall* be opened to us. And we begin to listen to His voice recorded by many of His disciples. Recorded in a book. But most of all we begin to listen to that same Voice within our own temple. And we never feel alone again.

***

95

[Jesus said]: If you have money, do not lend at interest, but give [them] to him from whom you will not receive them [back].

If your are in the process of finalizing your retirement plans, forget this advice. It does not concern you.

The idea here is, once again, that Jesus is drawing a parallel with spiritual life. We cannot collect interest on spiritual gifts. One simply doesn't collect interest on gifts, which we have also received for free. And drawing a parallel with material gifts, those that would not repay a loan are by far in greatest need of our bounty.

We must also learn to distinguish between giving and lending. Giving enriches our spirit, lending—our material coffers. A great mystic, a man called Paul Twitchell, once said: "To give and never to expect anything in return is the beginning of immortality."

But if we have been blessed (or cursed) with money, if having to administer material riches is part of the lesson we are to learn in this lifetime, then let us be grateful. Let us manage them wisely. Only under no circumstances can we allow ourselves to become attached to our money. We must ever remember that we are not the owners, only the stewards. After all, those who are on a spiritual path know that only that which is part of his or her state of consciousness is of any value. And that which is of spiritual value cannot be lost. You give it away, and you still got it.

If you don't believe me, try giving love. Or compassion. Or friendship. Or a smile.

And by the way. All gifts are spiritual.

***

96

Jesus [said]: The Kingdom of the Father is like [a] woman, (who) has taken a little leaven [(and) has hidden] it in dough (and) has made large loaves of it. Whoever has ears let him hear.

It is not what we have; it is what we do with it. We do not have to be incredibly talented, have a superb head for figures, nor be a master with words. Emmet Fox once wrote that the Bible can be explained in simple language. He was right. He must have put to shame scores of learned theologians. I came across his writings in 1982. Strangely enough, the first book of his I'd read had been first published in 1932, the year of my birth. The book made me think. Hard! It confirmed many of my suspicions. Fifty years had lapsed before I became ready to accept what Emmet Fox had to offer. Had I seen his book earlier, it probably would have left me indifferent.[115]

No matter. I am still grateful to him.

Emmet Fox had placed a little leaven in my consciousness. I hope the loaf I am offering will not give you indigestion.

***

---

[115]   Emmet Fox had written many books, including THE SERMON ON THE MOUNT, POWER THROUGH CONSTRUCTIVE THINKING, FIND AND USE YOUR INNER POWER, MAKE YOUR LIFE WORTH WHILE, DIAGRAMS FOR LIVING, THE TEN COMMANDMENTS et alii, mostly if not all published by Harper & Raw, Jew York, London.

97

Jesus said: The Kingdom of the [Father] is like a woman who was carrying a jar full of meal. While she was walking [on a] distant road, the handle of the jar broke. The meal streamed out behind her on the road. She did not know (it), she had noticed no accident. After she came into her house, she put the jar down, she found it empty.

Not an easy allegory.

The woman is, of course, the soul. The distant road is the spiritual life we embark on. It is distant, long, spanning many reincarnations. The meal in the jar is heavy but only to start with. It contains all the countless traits of her personality, a burden she has to carry. Yet note: she got rid of her load so gently, she didn't even notice *(For my yoke is easy, and my burden is light).*[116] She simply walked on until she finally arrived in her house, in the Kingdom of her Father. The jar was empty. She was free of her burden.

Jesus insists that the journey is not as hard as it seems. In fact, he claims the very opposite. After a while, it even becomes exciting. But we must pick up our jar and start walking. Soon it will be empty.

***

---

[116]   Matthew 12:30. Also see *logion 90*.

98

Jesus said: The Kingdom of the Father is like a man who wishes to kill a powerful man. He drew the sword in his house, he stuck it into the wall, in order to know whether his hand would carry through; then he slew the powerful (man).

The powerful man is none other than our ego. He who slays his ego will enter the Kingdom. He will be free of all attachments. He will test his sword on the various sheaths or walls of his house.[117] And then he will strike, in order to set himself free.

By the way.

No one can strike the blow but he or she who resides within his or her own consciousness (house). No one can do it for us. That's what makes it so tough.

***

---

[117]   The physical, mental and/or emotional sheaths.

99

The disciples said to Him: Thy brethren and Thy mother are standing outside. He said to them: Those here who do the will of My Father, they are My brethren and My mother; these are they who shall enter the Kingdom of My Father.

I do not believe that Jesus 'turned' on his relations. What I think this *logion* means is that in His eyes we are all on equal ground when it comes to entering the Kingdom. There are no favorites, no 'connections'. Providing, of course, that we do the will of His Father, the will of our Higher Self.

This question of His and/or our Father (or Higher Self) needs, perhaps, a word of elucidation. God is One. Soul is One. There is absolutely no difference between the Impersonal Divinity residing in your, mine or His heart. What differs is the level of consciousness that we have developed over the ages, which gives the immortal Soul its own individuality. In God we are all One, but each one of us shall forever, if he or she so chooses, remain an individual expression of that Oneness.

I never said it was facile.

On the other hand, it's really quite simple.

***

100

They showed Jesus a gold (coin) and said to Him: Caesar's men ask taxes from us. He said to them: Give the things of Caesar to Caesar, give the things of God to God and give Me what is Mine.

It is important to remember that Jesus invariably refused to get involved in what attitude we should have to those who are steeped in physical or material consciousness. On most occasions He simply ignored them.[118] He does not commit Himself whether we should or should not have money. Nor does He condemn anyone who is rich. What He does discourage very strongly is the *attachment* to money or indeed to any worldly possessions. He claims that where our riches are, our heart is, thus we make it harder for ourselves if we place our attention on things that are not of the Spirit. Respect for civil law, possession of worldly goods and all the appurtenances of the 'earth', or of material consciousness, are simply of no interest to Him.

Jesus' sole concern appears to be centered on the process of opening our eyes to our true nature. What we do with such knowledge, more often or not, He leaves to us. He gives countless examples of what His Father's Kingdom is like. Countless rather than one. We must find our own Kingdom. Not somebody else's, not even His. But one thing He makes abundantly clear. The admonition to *Give the things of Caesar to Caesar*, simply means that if we are to survive in this world we must obey the laws of the land. After all, we must survive in order to learn, and learn is what we have been born to do.

---

[118]   We find an example of this attitude in the statement: Let *the dead bury their dead*. (Luke 9:60). The dead are, of course, the spiritually not (yet) awakened.

As we progresses along the path of understanding, we find that all states of consciousness exist within very exacting sets of laws. Even as our scientists define the laws of the physical universe, we must gather and learn the laws of the astral, the mental and eventually the spiritual realities. Inasmuch as all these are best described as states of consciousness, they are each imbued with objective as well as subjective realities. The first step towards their discovery is the acceptance of their existence. A leap of faith. Then contemplation. Then... it's up to you. As Jesus had said so many times, the Kingdom is within *you*.

A note of caution.

The realities may or may not be subject to change, but our *perception* of reality, any reality, changes continuously during the process of becoming. In this sense, one could say that we are the sole creators of reality we abide in. Consequently, we have no one to blame for our particular circumstances but ourselves.

***

101

<Jesus said>: **Whoever does not hate his father and his mother in My way will not be able to be a [disciple] to me. And whoever does [not] love [his father] and his mother in My way will not be able to be a [disciple] to me, for my mother [......] but [My] true [Mother] gave me the Life.**

"Whoever does not hate... in *My way*..." In this context the word hate simply means a condition of *detachment*. Jesus is trying to explain the difference between physical (or emotional) love that breeds attachment to that which is 'worldly', and the Divine or detached or impersonal love that frees one from the guile of this world.

Parenthetically, I am tempted to suggest that in Biblical sense, the opposite of Love is power—not hate.

The last part of the *logion* refers to Jesus' *true Mother*, who gave Him the Life. We know that Jesus recognized Spirit as the sole progenitor of His State of Consciousness, thus here the *Mother* assumes such a role, to distinguish Her from His physiological, (or natural) mother.

***

102

Jesus said: Woe to them, the Pharisees, for they are like a dog sleeping in the manger of oxen, for neither does he eat nor does he allow the oxen to eat.

See *logion* 39.

People who admit to being anticlerical, who would dismiss all the priests (Pharisees) as the *dog(s) sleeping in the manger of oxen,* might do well to remember that Saul of Taurus, later known as Paul the apostle, began his journey as a Pharisee. There may well have been many others like him. Perhaps there are today.

Jesus warns us against Pharisees because by following the dictates of the leaders of various religious organizations we would unavoidably listen to and rely on the opinions of others: of priests, deacons, elders, bishops, monks, nuns, and many—perhaps well meaning—idealists, rather than to our own inner voice. The Kingdom is *within*—even according to the very religious proponents who, nevertheless, continue to interject themselves between us and our Higher Self.

***

103

Jesus said: Blessed is the man who knows i[n which] part (of the night) the robbers will come in, [.......] and gird up his loins before they come in.

Here the *night* is the dark side of the soul, the time we feel alone, sad, the time we loose sight of True (spiritual) Reality. In such moments the robbers, our negative thoughts, fill our consciousness and we enter a condition known to psychologists, and psychiatrists alike, as depression. As we progress on the spiritual path, we learn to recognize the symptoms of such adverse conditions and we prepare for them. We gird up our loins; we tell ourselves that all that is negative is transient, that there is always a new dawn even after the darkest night. Only God, Love, offers permanency, only Light is the source of all knowledge. Once we entrench these concepts firmly in our subconscious (soul), we are indeed blessed. We no longer fear the robbers.

***

104

They said [to Him]: Come and let us pray today and let us fast. Jesus said: Which then is the sin that I have committed, or in what have I been vanquished? But when the bridegroom comes out of the bridal chamber, then let them fast and let them pray.

In Hebrew tradition prayer and fasting have long been recognized as a form of punishment or penance. While others are having fun, the guilty ones must go and pray and fast. Such activity would normally be associated with weeping, mourning. No wonder Jesus asked his disciples what has He done to deserve such a sentence. It is evident that the disciples who advocated this exercise had been in need of placating their own consciences.

"But why drag me into this?" Jesus seems to be asking. "For as long as I rejoice in the Presence of the Father within me, for as long as He resides in my heart, how could I possibly be sad or mourning?"

This leads me to comment on perhaps the greatest misunderstanding of Jesus' teaching. There are some Christian religions that dwell on the Passion, the Crucifixion, on sin, on guilt, and generally indulge in some, if not all, forms of mortification. And all this in the name of Him who once said:

These things have I spoken unto you, that my joy might remain in you, and that your joy might be full.[119]

JOY! The whole purpose of His teaching is to make us happy, more happy. Not to teach us fasting, not to make us spend hours on our aching knees begging some distant, unknown deity to throw us a few scraps from his niggardly coffers. And furthermore,

---

[119]   John 15:11

He teaches us to learn the quality of joy that can never be lost, that can never be taken away from us. Emmet Fox once wrote: *Joy is one of the highest expressions of God as Life. Actually it is a mixture of Life and Love...*[120]

If we fail to be joyful, we fail to understand the very essence of Jesus' teaching.

***

---

[120]   Fox, Emmet ALTER YOUR LIFE, [Harper & Row, New York] pg. 123.

105

Jesus said: Whoever knows father and mother shall be called the son of a harlot.

We have only One Father and He is in Heaven. All else is prostituting our divine heritage. Jesus recognized only our spiritual nature. The only Father we are to know is Higher Self.

Note:
On 'earth', we subsist on compromise.
In spiritual reality, no compromise is possible.

***

106

Jesus said: When you make the two one, you shall become sons of Man, and when you say: "Mountain be moved", it will be moved.

See *logion 30 et al.*.

There is a trend to-day among some people to look for one's 'soul-mate'. Those seekers seem to spend a lot of their energy searching for the other half of their personality (soul?), not within their own psyche, but among the members of the opposite sex. It might be fun, but it will do nothing for their spiritual growth.

The two halves of our psyche are well and truly contained within the unique nature of every single human being walking this earth. The two are the conscious (the active or male) aspect of our personality, and the subconscious (the passive or female) aspect of that which we all are. Jesus assures us that when we reprogram our storehouse of information within our subconscious, when that which we think, and that which we thought in the past, becomes of a 'single mind', better yet: becomes a single, unified state, of consciousness, we shall have carried out our agenda.

It is rather like having to reprogram a computer, reprogram the countless megabytes of memory, which for a long time served the sole purpose of sustaining our body and soul together, but did not go beyond this phase.

In the Bible, Adam symbolizes this first stage of our evolution. Now, we are told to go beyond the phase of inherent dualism. We are told to strive to become one. Again, when we succeed, we

shall be able to raise our consciousness at will. We shall gain unlimited access to our High Self. We shall be able to say: I and my
Father are one.

***

107

Jesus said: The Kingdom is like a shepherd who had a hundred sheep. One of them went astray, which was the largest. He left behind ninety-nine, he sought for the one until he found it. Having tired himself out, he said to the sheep: I love thee more than ninety-nine.

See *logion 8* and *76.*[121]

A hundred ideas, a hundred philosophies, a hundred concepts. A thousand self-help books, ten thousand psychiatrists, a million preachers. Somewhere that one idea that really matters got lost.

No wonder.

There is a tremendous competition for our attention, our dollar. Think back. The one idea that really matters is there, at the back of your mind. In your secret place. Waiting to be rediscovered.

***

---

[121]   In the Bible, the *sheep* invariably symbolize thoughts or ideas.

108

Jesus said: Whoever drinks from My mouth shall become as I am and I myself will become he, and the hidden things shall be revealed to him.

...he that believeth in me, though he were dead, yet shall he live. And whosoever liveth and believeth in me shall never die. Believest thou this?[122]

If we believe in the above lines, then we will also believe this *logion*. If we do not, we are (still) dead. But if we even begin to believe, we shall live. We, who believe and follow His dictates, the words that come out of his mouth, we shall become as He is. Immortal. Omniscient. We have it in writing.

A tempting offer?

***

---

[122]   John 11:25-26

109

Jesus said: The Kingdom is like a man who had a treasure [hidden] in his field, without knowing it. And [after] he died, he left it to his [son. The] son did not know (about it), he accepted that field, he sold [it]. And he who bought it, he went, while he was plowing [he found] the treasure. He began to lend money to whomever he wished.

This is an object lesson about reincarnation. Still so many of us seem unaware of the Kingdom that exists within us. It lies buried under layers of misconceptions, under layers of mistrust in our potential, our capability. And as we move from one embodiment to another, the treasure within remains undiscovered.

This journey of Adam, of man steeped in the physical consciousness, goes on for a long, long time. There are many walking this earth today whose potential is still buried. And yet a day will come when our son, our own soul, ever on his journey, will stumble across the hidden treasure. Often by accident. Of course he would not find it if he didn't put his shoulder to the plow. That is a must. We do not know when or how we shall discover our Kingdom, but unless we seek, unless we knock, the door is unlikely to open. Not for thousands upon thousands of reincarnations. Not for millions of years.

So what? Aren't we immortal? So what's the hurry?

Well, there is some pressure to the process.

If selfishness is the greatest of sins, then surely, procrastination is a close second. Only the reality of the Spirit is unchangeable and thus eternal. As for the state of becoming, there are no guaranties that 'heaven and earth' will last forever. We read more and more about errant comets or asteroids taking theoretical potshots at our home. Anyone of those celestial fragments might put an end to the kindergarten we call earth. Man himself could annihilate this world by pressing the wrong button at the Pentagon. Were this to happen, then the souls which 'didn't make it' shall be absorbed into the Whole. One day a new earth would, no doubt, come into being. But the personalities of past cycles would be gone.

Forever.

It seems wise, therefore, to search for our treasure. It alone, we are told, is indestructible.

***

110

Jesus said: Whoever has found the world and become rich, let him deny the world.

If our entire wealth is material wealth, then we are better off denying such wealth. It would mean that we are lumbered with physical consciousness to the exclusion of higher aspirations. We need our physical consciousness for survival in this world. But that is all we need it for. We should deny dwelling in it any more than is absolutely necessary.

Our true home, our Kingdom, is not in 'this world'.

***

111

Jesus said: The heavens will be rolled up and the earth in your presence,* and he who lives on the Living (One) shall see neither death nor <fear>, because Jesus says: Whoever find himself, of him the world is not worthy.
    *Ms. literally: "and the earth is in your presence".

Evidently the translators had problems with this axiom, but the general meaning remains clear.

Jesus prophesies what happens to one who centers his attention on his Higher Self (the *Living One*). Such a person (a man, a woman, or child) shall witness, in a state of full consciousness, as his/her dual nature unites into a single state of higher consciousness.

Henceforth, such a person shall be beyond ever loosing his/her awareness of his/her true nature. The only death Jesus recognizes is spiritual death, and the only fear is the loss of the awareness of the Spirit within.

Finally, once we become fully aware of our divine nature, we are freed from all physical ties, from any and all attachment to the worlds of matter.

***

112

Jesus said: Woe to the flesh which depends upon the soul; woe to the soul which depends upon the flesh.

The flesh (or the body: physical, mental and emotional) is the sum-total of that which constitutes our personality. It represents the level of consciousness we have reached to-date. Some of us do not seem to realize that whatever we are today is the aggregate, the absolute summation of all our efforts over countless reincarnations.

This is as far as we got.

We cannot be anything else, because we made ourselves what we are. If we don't like what we see, we can change it. No one else can. We are gods within the extent of our subjective reality.

The soul is our subconscious (see other *logia*), or our memory bank, which helped us to get so far. We are told that the body, our physical survival, should not rely on knowledge already gained (but that it should draw its enlightenment from within, from the intangible). Likewise when attempting to reprogram our subconscious one should not rely on the experience to date, but we should be ever vigilant at recognizing, grasping and comprehending the whispers of our inner voice.

The best I can put it in today's language would be to say that one should rely on one's intuition rather than on one's instinct. Intuition, in this context, is that which enters our awareness from an 'unknown' source, the voice within, the often seemingly whimsical 'feeling' emanating from the unconscious, whereas instinct is limited to the automatic evaluation of the problems in the light of the acquired experience.[123] In other words, according to Jesus, we should always to be ready for a change.

It is indeed baffling, that people who will pay good money to see a movie in which the protagonist is continually challenged by ever mounting unknowns, are determined to make their own lives as predictable as possible.

Aren't we all actors on the stage of life?

The admonition: I *make all things new*[124] which John the Divine heard in his vision is not meant to be a one-time occurrence, but a state of consciousness which remains at all times receptive to the dictates of the Spirit. As our consciousness expands, so new concepts approach the range of our understanding.

***

---

[123]   As previously discussed, instinct is a reactive response to items of experience acquired over millions of years of evolution. Its function is *sine qua non* for survival in physical environment. In psychological terms it is a response to our subconscious. Genetically it is a reaction to the sum total of knowledge encapsulated in our genome. Mentally, it operates in an analytical/synthetic mode. Its job is to protect the *status quo*.

[124]   Revelation 21:5

113

His disciples said to Him: When will the Kingdom come? <Jesus said:> It will not come by expectation; they will not say: "See, here", or: "See, there". But the Kingdom of the Father is spread upon the earth and men do not see it.

It will *not* come by expectation. If we sit back and wait for it—good luck to us, only we shouldn't hold our collective breath. If we knock and keep knocking at the door—we are in better luck. At least we are on the right track.

The Kingdom of the Father is spread upon the earth, it is an integral part of that which we are; it is within the matrix of that which makes us human. It will not come after our death, nor shall we 'go' to it after we die. The Kingdom is a state of consciousness. It is a way of looking at things, at feelings, at ideas and ideals, at people.

In a way, it is an attitude.

It is also much, much more than that. It is a profound and absolute conviction, a total and unshakable confidence that Love, Compassion, Immortality, Omniscience, even Omnipresence are all unavoidable, irrevocable heritage of a human soul. It is first hand knowledge that these Divine qualities are already present in us all, that all we need to do is to open our hearts in order to experience them. People who sacrifice everything for the sake of what 'might be' are not studying Jesus' words. People who *live* His words are enjoying the benefits of the Kingdom right now. The Kingdom is here and now *and men do not see it.*

***

114

Simon Peter said to them: Let Mary go out from among us, because women are not worthy of the Life. Jesus said: See, I shall lead her, so that I will make her male, that she too may become a living spirit, resembling you males. For every woman who makes herself male will enter the Kingdom of Heaven.

The Gospel according to Thomas.

It is a man's world, run by man, for man etc., etc.. After all we are stronger, smarter, bigger, we can beat up any woman. Aren't we great? Can we really blame Simon Peter for expressing in words what some Christian churches continue to practice today?

Women are not worthy of the Life?

In the days of Jesus, women had been subservient, humble, and the Hebrew religion assured that they stayed that way. In some sects they still do. We are told that they (women) like it, that it is the will of God. What could Jesus do when faced with such bold ignorance? Had He declared equality of sexes, He would have been lynched from the nearest branch, possibly by his own disciples. He had to tread gently.

See, I shall lead her, so that I will make her male... Poor Mary. She must have been scared stiff. All these men, and the elder among them, Simon Peter himself, wants to send her away. (*I shall take her by the hand, I shall give her confidence. She will grow in self-assurance. She will learn to believe in herself... She will be as confident as any man*).

I shall make her male. I can see hordes of Christian fundamentalist gynecologists standing in line to implant the necessary prosthesis. Male???

Male or man or *Ra* is the symbol for the positive, conscious or active mind. The late Joseph Campbell said, in one of his lectures, that men must *do* things, women must just *be*. I would like to see a mother of four just 'being'! These are all symbolic representations. Woman, or wife, or *Is,* symbolizes the subconscious, the passive, the consolidating, the retentive. How very apt. Women symbolize—not are but *symbolize*—the gentler, nurturing aspect of our nature. We are *all* male and female. We even share most of the sexual characteristics. Even Popes have nipples. No matter. In some churches the symbol had long ago supplanted the substance.

...that she too may become a living spirit...

I can really feel for Jesus. Thousands of years of prejudice backed up by the word of God himself. Admittedly, an old-fashioned, vengeful God, but the only God around—at the time.

...resembling you males. (Resembling you ignorant lot who haven't understood a word I've told you. And you are by far the best of the bunch).

For every woman who makes herself male will enter the Kingdom of Heaven. Every woman who believes in her spiritual nature, who believes in her divine heritage, who believes in the omnipotence of Love, shall enter the Kingdom of Heaven.

One can but wonder how many males made it already, and how many women?

Any bets?

The Gospel
according to Thomas

Thank you Thomas. Thank you very much.

*****

BIBLIOGRAPHY

THE GOSPEL ACCORDING TO THOMAS. Coptic text established and translated by A. Guillaumont, H.-Ch. Puech, G. Quispel, W. Till and Yassah 'Abd Al Masih [Harper & Row Copyright © E.J. Brill 1959]

THE NAG HAMMADI LIBRARY Revised Edition. General Editor: James M. Robinson; (The Gospel of Thomas introduced by Helmut Koester and translated by Thomas O. Lambdin). Copyright © 1978, 1988 by E.J. Brill, Leiden, The Netherlands. [Harper Collins Publishers, 10 East 53rd Street, New York, NY 10022]

BHAGAVAD-GITA – AS IT IS – With translations and elaborate purports by (H.D.G.) A.C.Bhaktivendanta Swami Prabhupada. [The Bhaktivedanta Book Trust, Los Angeles 1976]

ENTERING THE STREAM Compiled and edited by Bercholz, Samuel and Kohn, Sherab Chodzin [Shambala, Boston]

Fox, Emmet *ALTER YOUR LIFE* [Harper & Raw, New York] For a list of his books please see page 153.

Pagels, Elaine *THE GNOSTIC GOSPELS* [Vintage Books Edition, January 1981. Copyright © 1979 by Elaine Pagels]

A Reader's Guide to the HOLY BIBLE, King James Version. [Copyright © by Thomas Nelson Inc. Camden, New Jersey 08103]

THE EDGAR CAYCE READER #2 Copyright © 1969 by the Association for Research and Enlightenment, Inc. [A Warner Communications Company].

THE COLUMBIA VIKING DESK ENCYCLOPEDIA, Third Edition, [Copyright © 1953, 1960, 1968 by Columbia University Press 625 Madison Ave., New York, N.Y. 10022].

THE SONG CELESTIAL OR BHAGAVAD GITA translated from the Sanskrit Text by Sir Edwin Arnold, M.A., K.C.I.E., C.S.I. [Self-Realization Fellowship, Los Angeles1999]

Young, Robert LL.D., *YOUNG'S ANALYTICAL CONCORDANCE TO*

THE BIBLE, [Copyright © 1970 by William B. Eerdmans Publishing Company]

Hoff, Benjamin *THE TE OF PIGLET* [Penguin Books, Copyright © Benjamin Hoff 1992]

Kapuscinski, Stanislaw *DICTIONARY OF BIBLICAL SYMBOLISM* [Inhousepress, Montreal, 2000, 2003]

Kapuscinski, Stanislaw *BEYOND RELIGION I.* A Collection of Essays on Perception of Reality. [Inhousepress, Montreal 1998, 2001, 2002]

Kapuscinski, Stanislaw *BEYOND RELIGION III.* A Collection of Essays on Perception of Reality. [Inhousepress, Montreal 2001, 2002]

*****

A Word about the Author

An architect, sculptor and prolific writer was educated in Poland and England. Since 1965 he has resided in Canada. His special interests cover a broad spectrum of arts, sciences and philosophy. His fiction and non-fiction attest to his particular passion for the scope and the development of Human Potential. He authored more than thirty books, nineteen of them novels and a few collections of short stories.

Under his real name he published seven non-fiction books sharing his vision of reality. He also composed two collections of poems in his original native tongue in which he satirizes his view of the world while paying homage to Bozena Happach's sculptures. His poetry in English, as well as a number of articles and short stories, can be seen at Authors Den: http://www.authorsden.com/stanislaw

If you enjoyed this book, please don't forget to write a (brief) review. I'm interested in your thoughts.

IP

INHOUSEPRESS, MONTREAL, CANADA
http://inhousepress.ca
email: info@inhousepress.ca

34017

www.ingramcontent.com/pod-product-compliance
Lightning Source LLC
Chambersburg PA
CBHW060241050426
42448CB00009B/1543